THE
KU KLUX KLAN
IN
KANSAS CITY, KANSAS

THE

KU KLUX KLAN

IN

KANSAS CITY, KANSAS

TIM RIVES

THE
History
PRESS

Published by The History Press
Charleston, SC
www.historypress.com

Copyright © 2019 by Tim Rives
All rights reserved

Front cover: Kansas Historical Society.
Back cover: Spencer Research Library.

First published 2019

Manufactured in the United States

ISBN 9781467142045

Library of Congress Control Number: 2019939732

CONTENTS

PREFACE

This book is an accident. In 1992, I was just a few weeks out of the army when I began working toward a graduate degree in U.S. history at Emporia State University. A seminar on "The United States in the 1920s and 1930s" under Professor Patrick G. O'Brien presented the first test of my research skills. Pat approved my idea to examine Depression-era rural churches to see what changes, if any, the deprivations of the era inflicted on their fortunes. A Methodist pastor in Reading, Kansas, kindly gave me access to her congregation's records. I found little that would distinguish a year in 1922 from one in 1935 other than accounting records. To my surprise—great is an understatement—I discovered numerous transactions from the 1920s recording payments from the local Ku Klux Klan (KKK) chapter for renting a church meeting hall. This discovery knocked the church idea right out of my head. I wrote my first graduate school research paper on the KKK in the 1920s, as well as my master's thesis a couple of years later. I've returned to the subject a few times in print, and now for a final time in this book.

The Ku Klux Klan in the 1920s, as you will soon see, was a massive social movement of otherwise normal, white, native-born, Protestant, middle-class Americans. The Klan lured them into its robes and masks with a promise to put the country right again, with them back on top. A reasonable observer might wonder where Klanfolk got the curious idea they were not "on top" at that point in the nation's history. But perception is reality, no matter when or where you live—or lived—including Kansas City, Kansas.

This book is based on records, especially those collected as part of two investigations. The federal government began investigating the KKK in 1921, when the Klan's sudden nationwide rise in membership and popularity shocked lawmakers. The federal investigation concluded without action when it was determined by the Justice Department that the potential violations of the law were likely at the local level. Some of the records that investigators collected were given to states like Kansas, which in 1922 began taking its own peek under the Klan's sheets. Abstracts of the records, as well as many fascinating exhibits, are held by the Kansas Historical Society. But best of all are membership rosters from a dozen Kansas cities, including Kansas City, found in the papers of former Kansas governor Henry J. Allen at the Library of Congress. The Kansas City membership roster names more than one thousand members, allowing this historian to identify Klansmen acting in newspaper accounts when no reference is made to their Klan membership. It's like a secret decoder ring. This advantage opened new lines of research that could not have been opened without knowing the secret allegiances of the men involved. The Grocer War of 1923 found in chapter 4 is just one example.

All Klan names are either from the membership rosters, newspaper accounts or testimony taken during the state's investigation of the organization. They have not been assumed by the author. The men whose names appear in the records are referred to as Klansmen throughout the narrative unless there is a specific reference to them leaving the Klan voluntarily or otherwise. Even those who were "banished" by the Klan still remained united in Klan political efforts. Although the Klan era was largely over by the end of the twenties, Klansmen are still referred to as such even thirty years later if their political activities remain in unison with other Klan members from the era.

Before pressing on with the rest of the story, a few points need to be made. The first is that *no* location identified in this book as a Klan meeting, business or dwelling place in the 1920s is in *any* way connected to the Ku Klux Klan today. Nor is anyone working or living in those structures, should the building still exist, in *any* way related to the Ku Klux Klan. Furthermore, there should be *no* assumption made about anyone living today who shares the same name as anyone identified as a Klan member in this book as having *anything* to do with the Ku Klux Klan.

Finally, I also wish to make clear that this book is not anti–Kansas City, Kansas. The city was not some racist or anti-Catholic aberration in the

1920s. The Klan was everywhere during the era. Kansas City would have been an anomaly to have avoided it. I hope this history is accepted as a gift to the people, past and present, of Kansas City, Kansas. It is a tribute to how the community has transcended a painful past and now sits at the greatest heights in its fascinating history.

One further point. Kansas City refers to Kansas City, Kansas, unless otherwise indicated.

ACKNOWLEDGEMENTS

L et's go back to the very beginning. I first learned about the Ku Klux Klan of the 1920s in an American history class with Dr. Patrick G. O'Brien at Emporia State University almost forty years ago. Pat's stories of these otherwise normal, middle-class Americans donning the white robes of the Klan to fight bootleggers, castigate adulterers and curse Catholics were as funny as they were unsettling. Dr. Loren Pennington was a great mentor at Emporia. Dr. Mel Kahn has enthralled political science students at Wichita State University for nearly fifty years. I was lucky to have been one of them.

A special thank-you to my fellow archivists and librarians around the world. What a great profession we share. Thank you, Anne Lacey, Kansas Collection librarian, Kansas City, Kansas, Public Library; Kathy Lafferty, copy services manager, Spencer Research Library; and Lisa Keys of the Kansas Historical Society for your critical help in locating and copying the many images I needed for this project. Thank you to Kaycee Anderson, North Platte, Nebraska, Public Library and Robin Garlett, St. Patrick's Catholic Church, North Platte, Nebraska, for helping me discover what happened to former Kansas City, Kansas mayor Harry B. Burton. The Library of Congress provides incredible online resources to researchers around the world.

Thank you to my National Archives colleagues, especially Mark Corriston, now retired, of the National Archives at Kansas City, without whom I would have never had a career in the stacks. Mark has also shared many stories of his native Kansas City and corrected my many misperceptions. Valoise

Armstrong and Mary Burtzloff of the Eisenhower Presidential Library alerted me to interesting archival items I was unaware of, as well as scanning and other digital advice.

Thank you to Loren Taylor, dean of Kansas City and Wyandotte County historians, for his services to his community's history. I especially thank him for pushing me to learn more about the Klan in Kansas City, Kansas, and for the opportunity to share my findings with the Wyandotte County Historical Society.

A special thanks to baseball historian Larry Lester and the Jerry Malloy Negro Leagues Baseball Conference for encouragement in pursuing the Tom Baird story. Writer friends Bill Kauffman, Jeff Zeter, Yanek Mieczkowski and Rich Helder have all, for better or worse, encouraged my writing on a multitude of subjects.

And now it's family time. There is simply no way to adequately thank such a loving and supportive clan, especially my wife, Susan; my parents, Robert and Priscilla Rives; and my children and their families: K.S., Eli, Rebecca and Amalia Revivo and Patrick Rives and Allison Burgess.

Thank you Lindsey Givens of Arcadia Publishing for this opportunity!

One of the best parts of the research was getting to know the many beautiful and historic parts of Kansas City, Kansas, and its environs. The rolling hills, the colorful neighborhoods and the pride of its citizens make me proud to be a Kansan.

Hat tip to St. Bede the Venerable.

INTRODUCTION

Like a prairie fire, a revived Ku Klux Klan (KKK) swept across the country in the early 1920s. Promoting "100 Percent Americanism, Law and Order, Protestant Christianity and White Supremacy," the new Klan quickly enrolled millions of Americans in a crusade to make the country in its image again.

A bewildering sense of loss fueled the mass enlistment. Where had the "old stock" American communities of the past gone? Why were immigrants rejecting traditional American values? Why did African Americans think they could move into their neighborhoods? Why did politicians repeatedly betray their interests? Why did scofflaws flagrantly violate their new prohibition law? Why? Seeking answers and action, native-born, white, Protestant Americans flocked to the hooded order.

The apparent *normalcy* (to borrow a word popularized by President Warren Harding) of the folk who joined the new Klan intrigued observers then and historians now. Unlike the neo-Nazis who claim the current Klan crown, members of the hooded order in the 1920s seemed like, well, normal, middle-class citizens—because most of them were. Klan robes rustled with small-business owners, railroad engineers, clerks and carpenters. They attended church. They frequented lodge meetings. They boosted their city. If one had to describe a typical member of the KKK in Kansas City, Kansas, Methodist, Mason and Republican would paint a pretty good picture.

The middling sorts were not alone. Prominent members of the 1920s Klan included Hugo Black, later a justice on the U.S. Supreme Court. Mount Rushmore sculptor Gutzon Borglum was a member, as was President

Left: Justice Klansman Hugo Black. *Library of Congress*.

Right: Mount Rushmore sculptor Gutzon Borglum publicly associated himself with the KKK. *Library of Congress*.

Harry Truman, however briefly. President Woodrow Wilson reportedly admired the Klan. Planned Parenthood founder Margaret Sanger spoke before an approving audience of the Women's Ku Klux Klan in 1926. President Harding was alleged to belong to the order, despite being joined to a Catholic wife. Tom Baird, the longest-serving executive and team owner in Negro League baseball history, was a confirmed robe filler in the Kansas City, Kansas *klavern* (chapter). The Ku Klux Klan of the 1920s also claimed the loyalities of senators and congressmen, governors and mayors, housewives and schoolboys.

The list of men, women and boys who joined the Klan was long. One indication of Klan strength was a march on Washington in 1926 featuring more than 30,000 Klansmen. "It was fantastic!" a Klan witness effused to the author. Kansas City held Klan parades, too, its marching columns embracing more than 2,500 white-robed Klansmen in 1927. An equal number of members cheered from the sidelines. The Kansas City Klan's annual Fourth of July picnics featuring Klan-themed beauty contests, baseball games, band concerts, barbecues, dancing, drill teams, patriotic orations and cross burnings, attracting tens of thousands of Klan members, admirers and interested onlookers.[1]

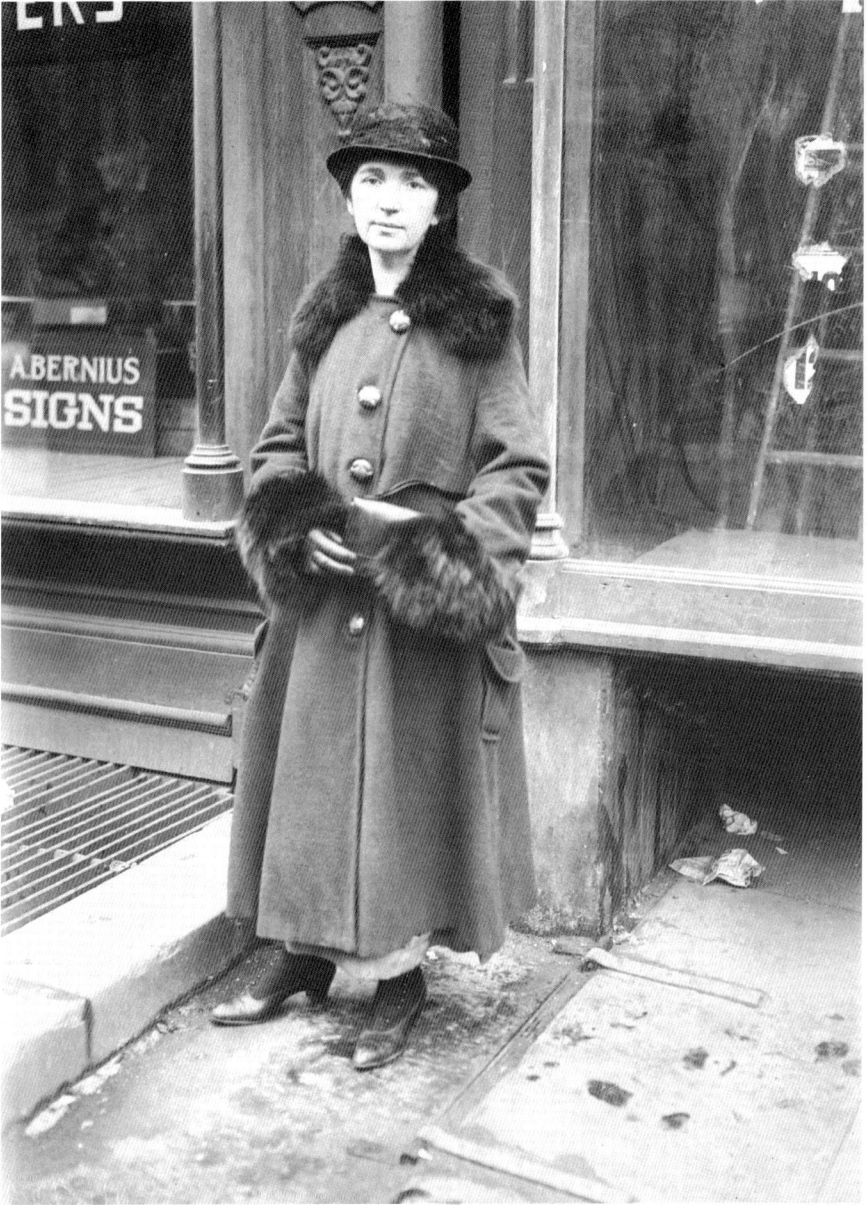

Birth-control champion and eugenics advocate Margaret Sanger spoke before an approving audience of the Women's Ku Klux Klan in 1926. *Library of Congress*.

Thousands of Klanfolk marched through Washington, D.C., in 1925. *Library of Congress.*

A general Klan craze engulfed the country. Klan fraternities rushed "Kappa Kappa Kappa" recruits on campus. Klan colleges sprouted up in Georgia and New Jersey. Klan orphans lived in "Klan Haven." Klanfolk enjoyed Klan movies, radio broadcasts and stage plays. A Klan flying corps patrolled the skies. A Kansas coed wailed, "Daddy Swiped Our Last Clean Sheet and Joined the Ku Klux Klan." The song was a hit.[2]

Most cities, including the nation's capital, required Klan marchers to remove their masks. *Library of Congress.*

The KKK of the 1920s was a madcap miscreant of history still difficult to comprehend nearly a century on. With its pilfered sheets, pointy hats and gauzy mumbo jumbo of Klanspeak, it is almost tempting to dismiss it as some goofy anomaly of the faddish Jazz Age, like marathon dancing or flagpole sitting. But to do so overlooks the damage done by the revived Klan, no matter how normal its members or admirers may appear or how

The madcap Klan of the 1920s included flying Klansmen. *Library of Congress.*

ludicrous its korny habit of turning every consonant *C* into a *K* may seem. The order harmed every community it "kluxed" (organized), including Kansas City, Kansas.

Consider the results. By the end of the 1920s, the men, women and boys who joined the Klan in Kansas City could look back with satisfaction on reversing the losses that had spurred them to action. Gone were offensive books from public library shelves. Fired was the Argentine High School teacher who promoted "jazz" dancing. Cancelled was the integrated school pageant. In rubble lay Catholic tombstones. Vacant stood homes once owned by African Americans in white neighborhoods. And captured was city hall, a trophy from the 1927 municipal elections. The Klan mayor and his inner circle would rule Kansas City for almost thirty disastrous years.

This book follows the rise and fall of the Ku Klux Klan in Kansas City from 1921 to 1930 and beyond. The narrative traces the tangled roots of Kansas City history exploited by the Klan, follows the order's noisy debut in spring 1922, reveals the Klan's destructive "methods and operations,"

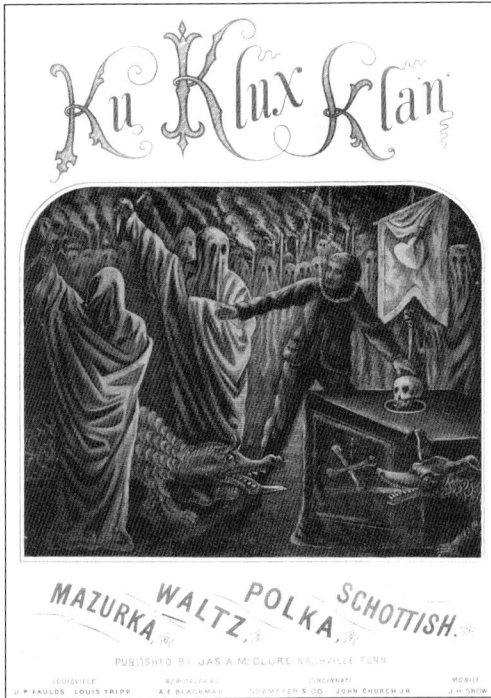

The Ku Klux Klan influenced popular culture from the beginning days of the order in 1865. *Library of Congress.*

probes its deep anti-Catholicism, unmasks the Klan's middle-class adherents, examines its drive for political power and chronicles its decline and eventual disappearance from Kansas City save for the members entrenched in city hall. It is above all a tale of otherwise normal people doing abnormal things.

The first Ku Klux Klan burst into American history after the Civil War. Founded by six former Confederate officers in 1865, the KKK was dedicated to terrorizing African American freedmen and women back into submission and resisting the political Reconstruction efforts of the federal government. The Klan's influence and violence quickly spread across the South, its power and lawlessness alarming officials, who finally brought it down in 1872 with the mass arrest and conviction of its members. Despite its dissolution, the Klan remained alive in the memory of many a romantic white southerner. And far from terrorists, the Klan's chivalrous knights were remembered as defenders of an imperiled white civilization.[3]

One of these romantic southerners, Colonel William Joseph Simmons, would resurrect the Klan in 1915. The "Colonel" (the title was strictly honorary) lay recovering in an Atlanta hospital from the wounds of an automobile accident when he experienced a vision to revivify the Ku Klux Klan. A former Methodist preacher and the son of an old Alabama

It took the power of the federal government to destroy the violent post–Civil War KKK. *Library of Congress*.

Klansman, Simmons was a district manager for the Woodmen of the World fraternal order when he conjured the Klan back to life.[4]

"On horseback in their white robes they rode across the [hospital] wall in front of me," Simmons dreamily recounted. "As the picture faded out, I got down on my knees and swore that I would found a fraternal organization that would be a memorial to the Ku Klux Klan." The fading picture was more likely painted in his mind by the epic 1915 film *The Birth of a Nation*, which heroized the work of the first Klan for a worldwide audience. "It is like writing history as lightning," President Woodrow Wilson said after watching the film, "and my only regret is that it is all so terribly true." Whatever its true inspiration, the idea to awaken the sleeping Klan giant was born.[5]

Later that year, on Thanksgiving eve, Simmons led fifteen recruits up Stone Mountain, Georgia, where they burned a cross and dedicated themselves to those "principles of Americanism embodied in the Constitution of the United States, consecrated themselves, as Protestants, to the tenets of the Christian religion, and pledged themselves, as white men, to the eternal maintenance of white supremacy." Simmons's "secret, social, patriotic, fraternal, beneficiary order" received a charter from the State of Georgia on July 1, 1916. The Ku Klux Klan was officially back in business.[6]

Historians still debate the effect of World War I (1917–18) on the new Klan's success. But the war apparently gave some impetus to Simmons's early organization as he succeeded in filling the ranks of the Citizens Bureau of Investigation (CBI) with his followers. The CBI secretly monitored local slackers, foreigners, radicals and others deemed harmful to the war effort. But despite the wartime service, the new Klan claimed only four thousand to five thousand members by 1920. Most of them lived in the South. The Klan might have remained a small regional organization without the intervention of Edward Y. Clarke and Elizabeth Tyler of the Southern Publicity Association.[7]

Clarke and Tyler sensed the Klan's potential as a national fraternal order—that is, as a money maker—and offered to market it across the

Colonel William Joseph Simmons revived the Ku Klux Klan in 1915. *Library of Congress.*

country. Simmons, an admittedly poor administrator and noted drinker, agreed. He took the money and removed himself to a mansion he christened Klan Krest. The title of Imperial Wizard bedizened his role as the monarch of the order until he lost the crown to Dr. Hiram Wesley Evans in a 1922 coup by men more interested in political power than Simmons's misty-eyed romanticism. Nevertheless, history marks June 7, 1920, as the day the "Colonel" signed the deal with Clarke and Tyler, and the Ku Klux Klan became an ascendant force in American life, breaking loose for the first time from its southern moorings and expanding its influence across the country.[8]

Clarke and Tyler (the pair were soon disclosed as lovers) commissioned a sales force of more than one thousand kleagles (salesmen) to peddle the Klan program. They expertly packaged the hooded order's restorative potential and sold it as the cure for the anxieties of the age. The pair also instructed their kleagles to "find out what was worrying a community and offer the Klan as the solution." This formula proved to be the genius of the second Ku Klux Klan: sell the hooded order as a broad national program for native-born white Protestant revival but let individual Klan chapters determine their own agenda based on local concerns.[9]

The Klan's successful recruiting under Clarke and Tyler's direction did not go unnoticed. The *New York Herald* began an exposé of the KKK in January 1921. The *New York World* followed in September. The *World*'s sensational reports on the Klan riveted Congress. Hearings ensued. In October, the U.S. House Rules Committee, chaired by Kansan Phillip Campbell (R), heard testimony on the Klan for more than a week but made no recommendations. Some observers interpreted the legislative silence as tacit approval of the Klan. "Congress made us," founder Simmons would boast. The efforts of the New York newspapers also served the Klan, as aspiring citizens of the "Invisible Empire" (as the Klan fancied itself) mailed in facsimile applications ripped from the papers. If the exposé had "increased *World* sales by a hundred thousand, it increased Klan sales by ten times that number," historian David Chalmers noted. The Klan's aggressive recruiting campaign, media interest and apparent government apathy resulted in an alleged gain of more than one million new members in little more than a year.[10]

The Ku Klux Klan arrived in Kansas City, Kansas, in early 1921 as part of the Clarke-Tyler expansion. Led by King Kleagle George T. McCarron, a provisional chapter known as the Sunflower Club was formed in February 1921. McCarron's kleagles found members in the

Form P-20R

CHARTER PETITION

Knights of the Ku Klux Klan

INCORPORATED

"The Most Sublime Lineage in All History"

TO HIS MAJESTY, THE IMPERIAL WIZARD, OF THE INVISIBLE EMPIRE, KNIGHTS OF THE KU KLUX KLAN (INC.), IN HIS AULIK IN THE IMPERIAL PALACE IN THE IMPERIAL CITY OF ATLANTA:—

GREETINGS from the undersigned native-born Civil Citizens of the United States of America, prompted by unselfish impulses provoked by the declarations of your "Imperial Proclamation;" each being a white male person of serious purpose who owes no allegiance of any nature or degree to any foreign government, institution, sect, people or ruler, over eighteen years of age, of good character, sound in mind and body and of respectable vocation;

Hereby most respectfully petition Your Majesty for citizenship in the Invisible Empire through a charter for a Klan to be located at_____

State of _____, Which we pray shall be issued to us, thereby vouchsafing to us the exalted privilege of extending the boundary of your beneficent dominion to the betterment of mankind and the happiness of humanity—"NON SILBA SED ANTHAR."

Left: A blank charter application awaiting the signatures of aspiring citizens of the Invisible Empire. *Author's collection.*

Below: The admission ticket to a Klan recruiting meeting outlines the order's principles as well as its interests in the applicant's occupation. *Author's collection.*

Form P-217—100M—2-6-23

"NON SILBA SED ANTHAR"

Your friends state you are a "Native Born" American Citizen, having the best interest of your Community, City, State and Nation at heart, owing no allegiance to any foreign Government, political party, sect, creed or ruler, and engaged in a Legitimate occupation, and believe in:—viz.

The Tenets of the Christian Religion.
White Supremacy.
Protection of our pure womanhood.
Just Laws and Liberty.
Closer relationship of Pure Americanism.
The upholding of the Constitution of these United States.
The Sovereignty of our State Rights.
The Separation of Church and State.
Freedom of Speech and Press.

Closer relationship between Capital and American Labor.
Preventing the causes of mob violence and lynchings.
Preventing unwarranted strikes by foreign labor agitators.
Prevention of fires and destruction of property by lawless elements.
The limitation of foreign immigration.
The much needed local reforms.
Law and Order.

REAL MEN whose oaths are inviolate are needed.

Upon these beliefs and the recommendation of your friends you are given an opportunity to become a member of the most powerful secret, non-political organization in existence, one that has the "Most Sublime Lineage in History," one that was "Here Yesterday," "Here Today," "Here Forever." Present this card at door for admittance, with your name, occupation and address.

Name _____

Occupation _____

Address _____

Discuss this with no one. If you wish to learn more, address Ti-Bo-Tim _____
"DUTY WITHOUT FEAR AND WITHOUT REPROACH."

Left: Klan membership application questions reveal the order's interest in a prospective Knight's heritage and beliefs. *Author's collection.*

Below: Signing this form made one an official member of the Ku Klux Klan. The receipt proved payment of the candidates ten-dollar "klectokon," or membership fee. *Author's collection.*

Wyandotte Klan No. 5 was just the fifth chapter in Kansas to be recognized by the new KKK. *Kansas Historical Society.*

city's small businesses, churches, factories, fraternal lodges, shops, union halls and rail yards. City hall and the county courthouse also supplied recruits. Following a "thorough combing of the region" for acceptable members, Wyandotte Klan No. 5, Realm of Kansas, Knights of the Ku Klux Klan (Inc.), the official name of the Kansas City chapter, received its charter from the parent Atlanta organization on February 17, 1922.[11]

The first group of No. 5 leaders was typical of the thousands of others who joined the Klan. Dr. DeVirda Houston Burcham was appointed as the klavern's first exalted cyclops (president). A serum company owner, Burcham was an active Mason, Baptist and Republican. Other klavern leaders had similarly respectable credentials. Klaliff (vice-president) Dr. Cresse P. Rhoads practiced dentistry. Klokard (lecturer) Walter H. Williams audited books for the Armour packing company. Kludd (chaplain) A.L. Nuegebauer drove a freight train. Klabee (treasurer) Jesse H. Baxter sold insurance. Klarogo (inner guard) Harry Lillich dealt groceries. Klexter (outer guard) Vic Potter policed the streets. Like Walter Williams, Klokan (investigator) W.H. Whisman kept books for a meatpacker. His brother Klokann (investigators) T.R. Taneyhill and C.F. White operated a drugstore and cut hair, respectively. Nighthawk (charge of candidates) J.W. Gill worked as a foreman.[12]

The Kansas City chapter's designation as Number Five meant that it was just the fifth Klan in Kansas to be recognized by the new KKK. Why did the Klan sell so easily in Kansas City? The answer is found in the next chapter.

1
THE CONTOURS OF LOCAL HISTORY

T he KKK's dual offer to revive the fortunes of the country's white Protestants and solve their local problems found plenty of buyers in Kansas City. The sense of loss that nurtured Klan growth in the city was emotional, but it was also real. The nation's complexion, if not its soul, had changed between 1890 and 1920, when a tidal wave of immigration crashed the nation's shores bearing twenty-five million newcomers on its crest. The numbers were not the worst shock. It was the composition. More than 80 percent of the newcomers were from southern or eastern Europe. Countries and regions such as Italy, Sicily, Greece, Russia, Poland, Czechoslovakia and Hungary provided the bulk of the new Americans, most of whom were Catholics, Jews or Orthodox Christians. The community Klan hall promised a return to a homogenous world free from the intrusions of foreigners, if only for one night a week and on special occasions. It was a safe place, a boost to the spirits and a haven from the fearsome changes of the new America. All was well within the hermetic world of the Invisible Empire. The Klan beckoned, and they came.[13]

Eligible and willing Kansas Citians eagerly accepted the Klan's promise to fix the city's problems, too. There were plenty of things to worry about in Kansas City, especially its powerful neighbor to the east, Kansas City, Missouri. It was a long, ongoing battle, stretching back to the mid-nineteenth century when Kansas City, Kansas, was still a cluster of five separate small towns and communities: Kansas City, Armourdale, Riverview, Armstrong and Wyandotte. The battle against the Missouri hegemon, however, could not be fully joined until an internal conflict was resolved. The dispute, the question, would linger in various permutations throughout the Klan era; to wit, cooperate or compete?[14]

Historically, those seeking cooperation were resigned to a second-class status. They envisioned the five communities strewn along the state line as a collective "Brooklyn" to Kansas City, Missouri's "New York." Their opponents denounced the deference of Kansas to Missouri interests. Kansans *must* meet their rival as an equal. Equality and independence required strength, and strength required unity.[15]

The forces of independence and equality won on March 6, 1886, when a new Kansas City, Kansas, was created with the consolidation of the five towns. Despite Wyandotte's predominant size, Kansas governor John A. Martin used his authority to select "Kansas City" as the new entity's name. "Kansas City," he averred, would sell more municipal bonds to investors than "Wyandotte." Choosing Kansas City over Wyandotte was an unfortunate choice that would hamper the development of an independent civic identity.[16]

Historian Leon Fink observed that at the time of consolidation "there were probably few more socially heterogeneous places in America than this industrial city on the edge of the prairie." Industrial demand was partially responsible for the city's ethnic and class variety. Kansas City's burgeoning meatpacking, railroading and manufacturing industries demanded a large labor supply. Workers came from around the world. Immigrants from southern, eastern and central Europe were drawn by both economic opportunities and faith communities. South Slovaks settled on Strawberry Hill, filling the houses and pews built by earlier immigrants. As older immigrants moved into commerce or up the management ranks, new immigrants filled their old jobs in the factories and yards.[17]

Public policy also contributed to the city's diversity by encouraging formerly enslaved African American "Exodusters" to settle in Kansas. An estimated twenty thousand African Americans arrived between 1878 and 1882. Many of them lived on the site of Quindaro Township, while others found land near Jersey Creek, an area dubbed "Rattlebone Hollow," and in "Cabbagetown" near Turkey Creek. Mexicans would begin to migrate to Kansas City in force during World War I to relieve labor shortages.[18]

As Kansas City and the nation adjusted to the new industrial order of the late nineteenth century, class tensions tightened in reaction to the tumultuous changes. Workers sought protection in solidarity, employers in order. Offering solidarity, the Knights of Labor found members and power

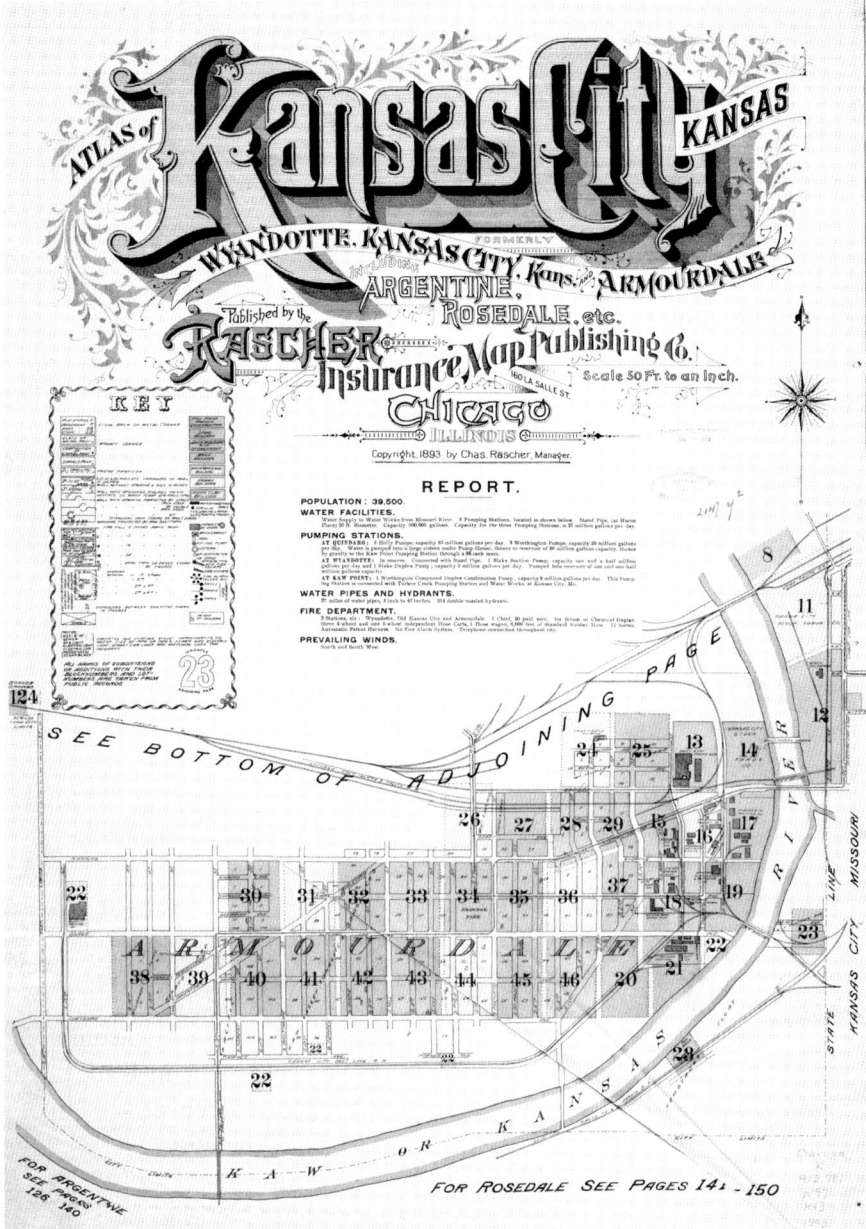

The 1886 consolidation of five smaller Kansas towns required a new atlas to guide visitors. *Kansas Historical Society*.

Morris Packing Plant, Kansas City, Kansas.

Above: Packing plants employed thousands of Kansas Citians, including dozens of Klansmen. *Kansas City Public Library*.

Right: The old courthouse served the new Kansas City. *Kansas City Public Library*.

in Kansas City. The union counted Mayor Thomas F. Hannan, the city's first mayor, as a member. While the Knights were devoted to the interests of workers, they embraced the republican principles and capitalist values of the nation's founders rather than the radical aims of the socialists and anarchists forming other unions. Nevertheless, the organizing success of the Knights in politics, as well as in the meatpacking and railroading industries (and their outrageous demand for an eight-hour workday) provoked a strong reaction from the business community. To rein in insurgent workers, 350 nervous members of the city's commercial class formed "Law and Order Leagues" dedicated to enforcing the prohibition of liquor more strictly, closing illegal gambling halls and abolishing labor unions.[19]

Fissures along religious lines widened with the influx of migrants, especially Irish Catholics like Mayor Hannan. The American Protective Association (APA), an anti-Catholic "patriotic" movement, flourished in the city from 1892 to 1897. Its propaganda was published locally in English and German versions. The APA's inclusion of foreign-born Protestants and African Americans (in separate lodges, of course) illustrates anti-Catholicism's appeal to a wide variety of Kansas City residents. The Klan would mine the city's anti-Catholic past when it came to town.[20]

Two issues dominated political affairs as the city entered the twentieth century: prohibition enforcement and the awarding of municipal contracts and franchises. The prohibition of alcohol—Kansas went "bone dry" in 1880—and its attendant law-enforcement problems frustrated Kansas Citians' efforts to build a city worthy of matching its Missouri neighbor. In 1903, angry citizens held mass meetings demanding stricter enforcement of the dry laws. The liquor issue forced Mayor W.W. Rose from office in 1905 for failing to shut the doors of the city's saloons. It was a tall order to keep Kansas City dry when booze flowed freely across the street from Missouri. And it was an even taller order, perhaps, to keep public officials from rewarding their friends with lucrative contracts.[21]

Reformers hoped changing the structure of city government would prevent future corruption. One measure they promoted after the Rose ouster was the city commission, a municipal model that elected representatives "at large" rather than by ward. The goal was "to take city government out of politics and enable capable men instead of vote getters." Although Kansas City voters approved the change in 1909, critics denounced it as elitist and undemocratic. Neighborhood divisions, village remnants of the city's pre-consolidation past, were still demanding a separate and equal say in city affairs. For years they had a say through their ward council representatives.

The councilmanic form of government, defenders claimed, allowed for a unified Kansas City without a complete centralization of power. Like anti-Catholicism, the commission/councilmanic conflict was another issue for the Klan to quarry.[22]

By the 1920s, the consolidation of the Kansas towns a generation hence had yet to build an independent metropolis to rival its Missouri neighbor. Liquor poured ceaselessly in city speakeasies. Labor and capital repeatedly clashed. Politicians wheeled, bickered and dealed time and again. The city's potential remained stubbornly unrealized.

Frustration with lingering problems from the city's past is evident in a series of articles published by the *Kansas City Kansan* around the time the Klan first emerged as a force in the community. The articles surveyed popular impressions of the city's civic and moral conditions. The responses repeat concern with the same issues of unity, law and order, progress and municipal independence of the previous forty years. Respondents criticized the lack of public accommodations such as water fountains, playgrounds and schools and the deterioration of sidewalks, alleys and streets. Garbage collection, transportation and weed control were also objects of complaint. "It's the weeds that give the city a 'rube' appearance," one citizen said. City government had failed to keep up with the times or the expectations of its residents.[23]

Residents wanted to see more civic pride, or local "patriotism," a concept of loyalty based on reciprocity, the lack of which undermined the local economy. "If the merchants of Kansas City offered for sale materials and stocks desired by citizens, would these citizens patronize their home stores, or continue to go to Missouri to spend their time and money?" asked a dubious booster.[24]

Kansas Citians demanded "fair play" in politics, their affairs conducted by "good men" with no interest in personal gain, and government operations run in a "business-like" manner. True to form, the Kansans demanded home rule. "Kansas City" (Kansas), ran a common lament, "is governed by Missouri politicians, political bosses. I know positively that a political boss in this town goes to Missouri, meets the political bosses there, and frames the program for our city." Kansans blamed their Missouri neighbors for practically every problem, from the stench of stockyard waste to furtive "petting parties" on the outskirts of town.[25]

Law enforcement, however, was the most distressing problem. "The trouble with this city," an indignant citizen charged, "is that the officials turn loose the criminals and bootleggers instead of making them pay the penalty for their crimes. It is a crime and an outrage against the community." Gangs waged open warfare across the county. Arrests climbed to record heights in 1922. Kansas City's large 21.5-square-mile size, its massive neighbor to the east, an inadequate police force, official negligence and a "large number of persons of foreign birth" were blamed for the quagmire.[26]

Kansas City's Protestant ministers offered the *Kansan* their analysis of the city's moral state. The clergymen blamed the recent war, lax parenting and misguided educators for the "decline in morals." The Reverend George W. Durham of the Metropolitan Avenue Methodist Episcopal Church warned, "The child in school and in the home is not taught to respect the Bible and its teachings, even as it was three decades ago. There is at present very little respect for the ten commandments, without which, moral degeneracy is sure to occur." Durham and his colleagues prayed the moral "pendulum will swing to more sane conduct in time." Perhaps it just needed a little help.[27]

Neighborhood leaders, including Durham's fellow clergymen, headed efforts to remedy the city's ills and the shortcomings of government with the formation of civic clubs and improvement associations. Led by the Reverend E.L. Brown, pastor of the Central Methodist Episcopal Church, the Armourdale Business Men's Club (ABC) was organized on May 1, 1920, just seven months before Klan salesmen arrived in the city. The ABC worked

Minnesota Avenue, Kansas City's "Main Street," around the time of the consolidation. *Kansas City Public Library.*

to improve its district with the addition of parks, swimming pools and a community house.[28]

The Sixth Ward Civic Club (SWCC) also represented Armourdale. The two clubs cooperated on campaigns to remove weeds, clean streets and ban carnivals, the latter because of the undesirable "floater" that trailed in its wake. Thomas C. Hattley, a garage owner, was president of the Sixth Ward club. The civic clubs' and improvement associations' other goals ranged from economic development to moral and racial restrictions.[29]

The civic improvement campaigns at the beginning of the 1920s, however, illustrate the city's tendency to divide rather than unite. Armourdale was riven with jealousy. The ABC and Sixth Ward Civic Club represented opposite ends of the same relatively small ward, but the clubs rejected a merger proposal put forward by Sixth Ward member William A. Callahan. The dissension prompted an Armourdale booster to muse whether "some political interests in another part of the city were endeavoring to keep a divided sentiment in Armourdale." The writer, *Kansas City (KS) Republic* publisher E.W. Wells, declared, "Just as long as there is found in Kansas City, Kansas, the need of numerous civic organizations to protect and foster the interests of the several divisions of the city, just that long will the city stand divided against itself. 'Without union in civic organizations there cannot be union in civic action.'"[30]

Thanks to the efforts of the Klan's kleagles, leaders of the ABC and the SWCC were soon united in the ranks of the Invisible Empire. It was a big, white tent. In addition to Reverend Brown and William Callahan, the editor Wells, Reverend Durham and the garage owner Hattley also found solidarity under the sheet. The Klan gathered strength as civic club leaders from across the city joined them. They included, among others, the following: John L. Zeller, president, London Heights Improvement Association; Dr. K.C. Haas, president, Argentine Activities Association; E.D. Cole and G.A. Hartweg, directors, Riverview Booster Club; and Tom Baird, director, Grandview Improvement Association.[31]

The need for unity and the civic progress necessary to become an independent metropolis was obvious to most Kansas Citians, not just prospective Klan members. But the direction that progress should take and the character of its program raised another important question. Who should lead? Two main groups battled for the right to determine this path. Their respective stances harkened back to the pre-consolidation debate over the response to the power of Kansas City, Missouri. The first group comprised local elites—dominant municipal politicians, industrialists and bankers—who advocated a program of intercity and interstate cooperation. Their "Greater Kansas City" agenda, critics charged, sacrificed Kansas liberty to Missouri interests. These men (and they were all men), leaders of the Kansas City Chamber of Commerce, the Kansas City Rotary Club and similar organizations, ensconced themselves in the city's central business district on Minnesota Avenue. Politically, they tended to support Kansas City, Missouri initiatives such as city commissions, city managers and other "progressive" measures backed by the *Kansas City (MO) Star*, a perfidious meddler in Kansas affairs, according to its critics.[32]

The local ruling class did little to counter its "disloyal" reputation. During a crime wave in 1922, business leaders such as O.C. Smith, president of the Kansas City Chamber of Commerce and of Kansas City Structural Steel, supported grassroots crime-fighting efforts, but "not for the purpose of criticizing certain agencies in Missouri....It is my opinion that the good citizens of the two cities and states are one in this matter." Smith's fellow businessmen formed a Kansas branch of the "Law Enforcement League." Led by President James H. DeCoursey, a prominent Catholic and creamery owner, and Secretary Albert Mebus, a druggist, business leaders flocked to the Missouri-based organization. "The committee will make a great mistake," warned Kansas City, Kansas police chief Henry T. Zimmer, "unless it extends its influence to bring about observance of the law in addition to the enforcement of it." The chief "cited the fact that the 'enforcement organization' in Kansas City, Mo., is charged with being merely a political creation of selfish propagandists who are endeavoring, it is said, to extend their influence over this city."[33]

Opposed to the cross-state compromisers and the influence of the reviled *Star* stood a second group of Kansas Citians. Longtime Republican politicians of the city's conservative "stand pat" faction and small-business owners dominated this faction, although they were not alone. Democrats and workers of every trade could share their sentiments. These men advocated economic and political autonomy, not cooperation—or, in their view, cooptation by their Missouri rivals. This camp found much of its spirit on the city's south side, along Kansas Avenue, the city's "second" business district in Armourdale. But if establishment leaders looked across the state line for direction, key members from the anti-Missouri group responded with a shake of the secret hand of the Ku Klux Klan. "100 Percent Americanism, Law and Order, Protestant Christianity, and White Supremacy" would be both the foundation of their plans for the city and the bond of their solidarity.[34]

Kansas City proved a good opportunity for Klan organizers. The kleagles quickly discerned the historic worries of the city—the hegemony of the other Kansas City, the divided interests, the lack of progress—and sold the Klan as the solution to the problems. Wyandotte Klan No. 5 would give its members a united voice of protest and a path to power. Combine the local agenda with the KKK's wider campaign for white Protestant revitalization, and the reason those otherwise normal Kansas Citians donned the Klan's frightful habiliments is explained.

Before establishing an official Klan hall at 747 Minnesota Avenue, No. Five met at various locales. The Grund Hotel at 806 North Sixth Street was the site of early meetings and initiation ceremonies. Other Klan conventicles included the "Old Armory" at 845 Minnesota Avenue and a building at Thirteenth and Troup Streets. After a year of clandestine preparation, Wyandotte Klan No. 5 stood poised to move out of the lodge and into city life.[35]

2

CRASHING THE CITY

Kansas City heard the first swish of Klan sheets in December 1921, when the *Kansas City Kansan* published this letter from Wyandotte Klan No. 5: "Dear Sir: Please find enclosed fifty dollars ($50.00), which we ask that you kindly hand to the widow of Rev. A.J. Morton, deceased, explaining that is from Kansas City Klan No. [5], Knights of the Ku Klux Klan: the members of which extend their heartfelt sympathy to the family in their hour of bereavement. Very truly yours, Knights of the Ku Klux Klan."[36]

The *Kansan* delivered the donation to Mrs. Morton. "She expressed her thanks, saying she appreciated the spirit in which the money was given more than the money," the paper reported. What she did not say, because perhaps she did not know, was that the late Reverend Morton was a member of the KKK, as were numerous employees on the *Kansan* staff.[37]

While the Klan undoubtedly wanted to assist Mrs. Morton, the real message of the donation was ominously clear: The Ku Klux Klan is here, and we're here to help. Like it or not.

This was the moment city leaders feared. The KKK was already known to local authorities thanks to the wide circulation of the *New York World* and *New York Herald* investigations. Mayor Harry B. Burton first voiced alarm over the Klan's possible presence in Kansas City in July 1921. "We will treat the Ku Klux Klan as any other mob," Burton pledged, "should it start anything in Kansas City." Burton's chief of police promised to "break it up and prosecute its members" if the Klan attempted to form a "den" in

Leavenworth, Kansas Klansmen on their way to a gathering of the Klans. *Kansas Historical Society*.

his town. But the mayor and chief remained curiously silent following the *Kansan* article, as did the Klan. Reports of kluxer activity disappeared from the news over the holiday season. It was not until the next spring that the order reappeared in the papers.[38]

Mrs. Arnold Botterson of 2041 Tremont Street was alone late one night in March 1922 when she saw twenty-five white-robed figures emerge from four automobiles at the intersection of Stewart Avenue and Tremont Street. The "party moved so silently it is believed no one living on the street but those who happened to be awake and observing the street at the time were aware of the white-robed pedestrians," the *Kansan* reported. The mystery men split into two parties as they approached the top of the hill on Stewart Avenue before disappearing from Botterson's view. Mrs. E. Lewis, who lived across Tremont Street from Botterson, saw the "night riders" descend. Neither woman informed the police of the midnight march, turning to the newspaper instead; a neighbor edited the *Kansan*. Nor did they see what the Klan was up to on the hill. Houses from the era still stand at the crest, so the trip was not to an empty lot for a rally or an initiation ceremony. The mystery endures.[39]

Twenty-five robed Klansmen emerged from automobiles at the intersection of Tremont Avenue and Stewart Street in 1922. The men disappeared over the crest of the hill. *Author's collection.*

386. NORTH TREMONT AVENUE, FROM PARALLEL AVENUE, KANSAS CITY, KANSAS.

A postcard from the area of the Klan's ascent up the Stewart Street hill shows what the neighborhood looked like in the 1920s. *Kansas City Public Library.*

News of the Klan's nocturnal ramble up the Stewart Avenue hill alarmed Mayor Burton, as his fears of the previous year rematerialized. Speaking to the city's Ministerial Alliance at a meeting of the chamber of commerce in April 1922, Burton warned the clergy against "any organization whose activities tend to create prejudice in Kansas City against Catholics and colored persons." But the Klan's next reported act was merely the delivery of flowers to the home of Sanford Hamilton. An electrical lineman, Hamilton had fallen to his death from a utility pole at Twelfth Street and Park Avenue. "How the pillow [of flowers] with its Ku Klux Klan emblem came to be with the other flowers, has not been learned," the *Kansan* reported. Kansas City Klansmen accompanied Hamilton's body to his McAlester, Oklahoma funeral. Clad in full Klan regalia, the six Kansas City "Klansmen carried a blood-red carnation and at the close of the Masonic service dropped the flowers into the grave." The service marked the first appearance of robed Klansmen at a funeral in McAlester, the paper noted.[40]

The late-night maneuvers and funeral visits were only the beginning. Klan No. Five was ready to make itself even better known to the city and its officials, and in dramatic fashion. On April 22, 1922, five masked and robed Klansmen interrupted services at the Metropolitan Avenue Methodist Episcopal Church to present the Reverend George W. Durham with a cash donation and a letter of appreciation thanking the pastor for "his patriotic addresses…advocating civic justice and political equity." Durham invited the men forward to address the congregation. The Klansmen boasted that their organization comprised seven

Kansas Klansmen giving the Roman salute to new citizens of the Invisible Empire. *Kansas Historical Society*.

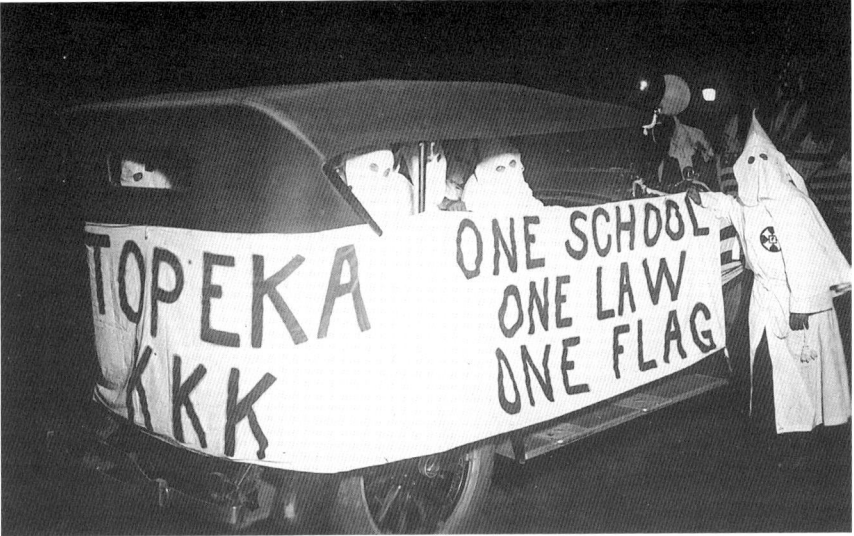

Topeka, Kansas Klansmen publicizing their program of 100 Percent Americanism. "One School" meant no parochial schools. *Kansas Historical Society*.

thousand "One Hundred Percent Americans" in the city and represented "everything that is good and clean morally, righteously, and politically," before taking their leave. The visit to Durham's church was just the second sighting of the Klan in public north of the Mason-Dixon line, according to the papers.[41]

The carefully planned church visits continued throughout the spring. After Reverend G.C. Schaub of the Trinity English Lutheran Church received a Klan donation, "the lights went out and a motion picture machine flashed the Stars and Stripes on a curtain [in] back of the pulpit. The congregation sang 'America' and the five men left," a well-choreographed act suggesting foreknowledge of the call.[42]

Reverend David T. Cruden of the Quindaro Boulevard Christian Church was an eager pastoral greeter of the Klan. "I am behind an organization with those ideals and will aid it anyway I can," Cruden said as he informed his congregation of the Klan's donation. Cruden is revealed as a member in the records of Wyandotte Klan No. 5, an interesting association given his Scottish birth and the Klan's official insistence on native-born American membership.[43]

Other Kansas City churches took a more guarded stand on the Klan. The Reverend J.K. Harris of London Heights Baptist Church spoke on the

Klan's entry into the community in early May. Harris challenged the Klan to "come before the ministerial alliance and declare their purpose and prove their loyalty to truth and justice, [and] acknowledge their faith in lawful assemblies." Reverend J.M. Mason of the Quindaro Methodist Episcopal Church invited the Klan to speak at his church "at the suggestion" of unnamed authorities. He reported that Klansmen were present, but none accepted his call to address the congregation.[44]

Reverend G. Franklin Ream of Washington Avenue Methodist Episcopal Church refused to accept the Klan's cash donation unless the men removed their masks. Ream would soon emerge as a Klan opponent, openly denouncing the order from his pulpit over the summer of 1922. The men left with their faces shrouded.[45]

Ream's rejection of the Klan was mirrored by the city's African American congregations. The Klan visited nearly "every colored church" and donated ten dollars, an act the *Kansas City (KS) Sun* wryly noted showed "that while they may be opposed to the African race 'running the earth' they are not averse to aiding them in their efforts to reach heaven."[46] The Klan explained the purpose of its visit in a letter to an African American church:

> *We are very much aware that some persons with selfish ambitions have addressed your people and have sent letters among them telling of our dislike for the colored race. But right here let us say that our membership is 100 per cent American and we are always friends of good law-abiding citizens white or colored. We are watching and aiding every good American institution and our investigations have proved your church is such and a credit to our city. We wish to express our appreciation to all law-abiding citizens.*[47]

Reverends D.B. Jackson of Eighth Street Baptist Church, T.A. Bowers of St. Peter's Methodist Church and P.A. Morrow of First Methodist Episcopal Church handed the Klan gifts over to charity; other church leaders returned the money to the Klan.[48]

On May 1, 1922, Kansas City Klansmen made their largest donation to date, $402, to Bethany Hospital. "This is a token of our appreciation for what you are doing for the poor of this community," Klansman Paul Taneyhill said from behind his mask. The African American Douglass Hospital received a drastically smaller token of $25, while the Catholic hospital received none. Wyandotte Klan No. 5 would also support Wilson

Bethany Methodist Hospital, Best equipped Hospital in Southwest, Kansas City, Kansas.

Wyandotte Klan No. 5 made its largest charitable contribution to Bethany Hospital. *Kansas City Public Library*.

High School with a pledge of $200. The Klan revered public education as a bulwark against such "un-American" community influences as parochial schools, which it later pressured lawmakers to outlaw.[49]

The church and hospital visits served several purposes for the Klan. First, it announced the Klan's "benevolent" presence in Kansas City; second, it linked the Klan with the Protestant churches, hospitals and public schools; and third, it attracted recruits. Intimidation of the "Catholic, Jew, Negro, thug, gambler, bootlegger, prostitute and other people of that character"—a Klan official's depiction of the order's enemies—was the darker goal of Klan charity.[50]

With those enemies in mind, Exalted Cyclops Burcham announced, "This is a law enforcement organization. I wish you to get that clear." The Ku Klux Klan's idea of a well-ordered society linked moral rectitude to a city's fortunes. Public order and civic progress were predicated on private virtue. Hence, the enforcement of law, especially the prohibition of alcohol, was a moral and political necessity for Kansas City Klansmen. Sober citizens made the best citizens. To keep them that way, the Klan hired private prohibition detectives from Wichita to help police round up bootleggers and destroy stills. The hired men, however, would soon leave town over a pay dispute, claiming the Klan had stiffed them.[51]

More often, the Klan did its own detective work. Wyandotte Klan No. 5 encouraged its members to "go around pool halls and gambling places where [criminals] loaf and report what they hear." Klansman John L. Zeller explained: "The members are admonished to observe the general conduct of the citizenry and report to the Cyclops or his appointed representative any violations of the law, or any acts that lead to the violation of the law... if it proves of merit it is taken over to the police department, the prosecuting attorney or the sheriff's office." The Klan's biggest tip involved a "yegg"—a safecracker—whose arrest yielded "a money bag stolen from the American Lunch, a number of peculiar looking little tools, and old rags, apparently to deaden sounds," according to Zeller.[52]

The Klan also functioned as a national spy network. Following tips from other Klans, No. 5 members tracked wanted men from Georgia, Oklahoma and Kansas. Exalted Cyclops Burcham described how the process worked: "We had a letter from an organization in Oklahoma that a certain Jew had come to Kansas City, and they wanted us to locate him, and if he was there to notify them, and they would send an officer and take him back. We failed to locate the Jew. He was not in Kansas City, at least we did not find him." Jews, who predominated the Klan's list of wanted men, were all charged by the hooded order with allegedly abusing women.[53]

Local reprobates proved easier prey. Klan No. 5's complaints against the Reverend David T. Cruden forced him from the order despite his support of the Klan before his flock. His overt support of the Klan likewise forced him from the pulpit. He left Quindaro Christian Church for independent evangelical work. The Scotsman had faced hardship before. He had spent six years in the far reaches of Ontario—"sixty miles past the edge of civilization"—ministering to lumberjacks. On Sundays, Cruden would "mount his dogsled, drive miles, pull into a lumber camp, feed his huskies at the cook-shack door and deliver his sermons across a log." Cruden survived attacks by black bears and wolves in the north land. Heart problems proved too much, however, and the former Klansman died in 1924 while scribbling a note to his wife describing the symptoms of his pain.[54]

Law enforcement and moral comportment were important to the Klan, but politics held the main prize. As Imperial Wizard Hiram Wesley Evans said, "By no other means can most of our demands be accomplished." The Klan's first move was on city hall. When Kansas City Water and Light commissioner L.H. Chapman submitted his resignation in June 1922, No. 5 plotted to dictate the selection of his successor. Chapman and Mayor Burton were allegedly tied to Thomas A. Bigger's "city hall machine." The machine, it was rumored, worked in the interests of Kansas City, Missouri, and was controlled by the *Kansas City (MO) Star*. The Missouri paper and Bigger were not the only issues to the Klan, however. Chapman hinged his resignation on the condition that he be replaced by city engineer James D. Donovan, a Catholic. Donovan's religion was the larger issue to the Klan. In the event, Chapman decided to remain in office rather than start a religious war. The incident announced the arrival of new political power in Kansas City and, with it, a surprising tactical alliance.[55]

African American Republicans supported the Klan's opposition to Donovan. As unlikely and illogical as it may seem, they and white Republican Klansmen remained political allies throughout the Klan era. "Issues," a realistic African American leader explained, "are uncertain and unsubstantial things in the hard world of necessities. We have been juggled and befogged on issues too many times. What we want is not issues, but jobs." Maintaining their place in the Republican Party meant retaining their small share of patronage jobs, no matter how menial the position.[56]

Klansmen, however, were singularly "juggled and befogged" with issues, issues of power, probity, class and race. Led by Reverend George Durham, three hundred concerned Klan citizens demanded the board of education dismiss the Argentine High School dancing instructor. "Some of this dancing has been called folk dancing, but what do you call it when I saw a group of young folks in our high school playing jazz music and waltzing to it?" Durham asked. The school's spring pageant also angered Klan parents. "It was a tax on poor people," Durham charged, "and many of them could ill afford to spend the money it cost to dress their children properly for the occasion." Even worse for an organization dedicated to white supremacy, Superintendent Dr. Matthew E. Pearson planned to racially integrate the pageant until a delegation of Klansmen convinced him to cancel his plans. Political alliances with African Americans were one thing; social mixing was quite another.[57]

The Klan's jarring masked and robed pursuit of all that it considered "good and clean morally, righteously, and politically" soon forced city leaders to action. Mayor Harry B. Burton announced on April 24, 1922:

> *I believe America and Kansas City are big enough to house all classes, creeds and colors in harmony. I believe in laying cards on the table and in the revealing of identities in any organization and I do not believe any organization ashamed of its identity should be permitted to instill fear into the hearts of other people who might otherwise function as good citizens. Being a real American, to me, means toleration of all.*[58]

The next day, the *Kansan* trumpeted the bold headline, "Burton Launches War on Ku Klux." The mayor's war on the Klan would rage for the next year. A Democrat, Burton, born on October 12, 1887, at Climax, Kansas, was elected mayor of Kansas City as the Union-Labor candidate in 1921. A Protestant and Mason, Burton had nevertheless appointed a well-known Catholic, George H. West, as police judge and hired four Catholic police officers. "His fairness to Catholics since taking office a year ago has been utilized by his political enemies to arouse feeling against him," the *Catholic Register* reported. "It is well known the Klan is being organized by his political enemies and intends to back its own candidates at the next county and city elections."[59]

Burton's alleged affiliation with a certain Kansas City, Missouri newspaper also angered the militant localists who enlisted in the Klan. Not only were Burton's political ties suspect to No. 5, so also was his membership at Washington Avenue Methodist Episcopal Church, whose pastor, G. Franklin Ream, refused the hooded order's donation. Moreover, fearing civil disorder, Burton had already forbidden the Klan to march in an American Legion parade, an organization fairly dominated by Klan members. The brief history between Burton and the Klan was marked by mutual suspicion and antipathy. It would go downhill from there.[60]

Mayor Burton attempted to mobilize public opinion against the Klan with an open letter to the citizens of Kansas City in which he decried the order for setting "neighbor against neighbor" and fanning the "flames of prejudice." But Burton also recognized the genuine concern for the city that had led some of the men into the order. He appealed to them on civic grounds:

> *To those of you reluctant to quit under fire, I would answer that your first interest, and your highest responsibility, rests upon you as a citizen of Kansas City and not as a Klansman. Your desire to bring peace and harmony into this community should overcome your reluctance to disband under criticism. I send this call to your community spirit, your love for Kansas City and not to your personal pride.*[61]

The mayor then shifted to the administrative front, where he requested all city employees who were Klan members to renounce their membership in the Invisible Empire or risk the loss of their jobs. Burton's threat "occasioned considerable levity" among city workers, of whom nearly fifty had already joined the hooded order. Although all four city commissioners eventually endorsed Burton's anti-Klan measures, Commissioners Kaelin and Strickland questioned the city's right to proscribe an employee's off-duty associations. As if to confirm Klan founder William Simmons's boast of federal approval, Kaelin argued, "I have seen in the papers where it was recognized by congress." Nevertheless, the commissioners proclaimed a state of emergency to protect the "peace and happiness" of the city. To that end, they passed an ordinance prohibiting the "appearance in public of any person in any costume which conceals his identity." Soft-pedaling the ban, Mayor Burton assured Klansmen that the anti-mask law protected them "in that it would prevent crooks from adopting their disguise and preying on the people or in gratifying of personal grudges."[62]

Burton's first three assaults on the Klan—official condemnation, administrative fiat and prohibition of masks—compelled the order to defend itself. On May 1, 1922, Wyandotte Klan No. 5 challenged the mayor to debate the Invisible Empire's merits. Klansman John L. Zeller, men's Bible class teacher at London Heights Methodist Episcopal Church, arranged the contest there between the mayor and "Dr. Harry Graham," an

Mayor Harry B. Burton debated Klan spokesman "Dr. Harry Graham" at London Heights Methodist Church in May 1922. The building still stands at Fifteenth and Garfield. *Author's collection*.

alleged Boston-based Klan lecturer. He was in fact Dr. Harold A. Bullard, an Independence, Missouri dentist turned Klan activist. Why he insisted upon the *nom de klan* was not revealed.[63]

Two thousand spectators crammed the church at Fifteenth and Garfield Streets on May 7, 1922, to watch the debate. Spectators filled every windowsill and aisle. Hundreds more gathered outside. ("The collection," the *Kansan* winked, "was not omitted.") Dr. Graham enjoyed a home field advantage. More than twenty Klan families belonged to London Heights. The audience greeted Graham with applause but offered only a chilly silence to the mayor, despite the "uncomfortably hot" conditions of the auditorium noted by reporters. The room hummed with tension as the opponents made their opening remarks.[64]

Graham welcomed the mayor's attack on the Klan, as the "more said against us, the more men flock to our standard. The riffraff of the country cannot get into our organization. The men whom we take in are the best men of every community, men who are respected, fearless, and courageous." Graham asserted that the country needed the Klan because of widespread "moral degeneracy and political debauchery." Government had failed. Politicians were for sale. Those were givens. But women and children required the Klan's special attention and protection, the dentist said, "the sanctity of the home…being violated a thousand times a day." For proof he cited the 70,000 illegitimate births since World War I, 40,000 of which were born to mothers younger than fourteen years of age. Moreover, 200,000 Americans had died from cancer in the last year. Of these cases, 40 percent "were traceable to social diseases," he asserted. "Keep your sons and daughters off the streets," Graham warned. Civilization depended on it.[65]

Burton, like other anti-Klan officials, based his opposition to the order in large measure on its secrecy. "Why do they clothe themselves in secrecy and go about their work in the dead of night? Why do they wish to take the law unto their own hands? We have the ballot to change conditions when they are wrong.…Let the Klan dispose of its robes and hoods. Let members show their faces," Burton said. Also like other anti-Klan officials, Burton opposed the Klan's challenge to the state's exclusive claim on legal power. "No man or body should take the law unto his own hands. Let there be due process of law." The Klan should not attempt to substitute itself for government.[66]

Burton was right, but he did not stand a chance against the audience or the charismatic Klan crusader. The *Kansan* fairly gushed in its depiction of "Dr. Graham." "He did not appear any different from hundreds of others in the church, except, perhaps, for a certain intensity of gaze, an alert, direct

The Ku Klux Klan initiating new citizens into the Invisible Empire on a baseball field in Mississippi. *Library of Congress.*

expression of the eyes." A starstruck boy said, "Gosh, don't his eyes look at you!" How could the mayor have possibly won against an opponent whose "personality might best be described as dynamic"? He couldn't. The entire event was a setup.[67]

The *Catholic Register* reported, "The audience, which besides being anti-Catholic and pro-Klan, was also very much anti-Burton." Hostile Klan fans hissed the mayor. "Before an audience of intelligent thinking men, he [Graham/Bullard] would be no match for Mayor Burton's straightforward logic, but before an ignorant anti-Catholic audience such as attended the debate, he had the best of the mayor." And he had it across the country when wire services picked up the story.[68]

Despite his poor reception at the London Heights debate, Burton's continuing war against the Klan was winning approval in the community. On May 6, 1922, the day before the debate, Burton introduced an anti-Klan resolution to the Wyandotte County Democratic Convention: "That the constitution of the United States provides equal rights to all citizens regardless of race, color, or creed, and that we, Democrats of Wyandotte county, stand opposed to any organization which includes hatred or prejudice among our citizens," the statement read. The Democratic Party support of Burton's "crusade against the Ku Klux Klan" and an approving *Kansan* editorial (despite its fawning over Graham) appeared along with coverage of the debate to strengthen the mayor's position.[69]

Burton had landed another punch two days before the debate when a "semi-official" investigation of the Klan resulted in the arrest of Klansman Melvin T. Puckett. Guarding the entrance to a Klan meeting at the Old Armory, Puckett was arrested on vagrancy charges by Police Judge George H. West, Chief of Police Henry T. Zimmer and four other officers. Klan attorneys William L. Wood and Louis S. Harvey represented Puckett the next morning in court. Tempers erupted. Wood, a prominent Mason, Republican and former Texas cowboy, lashed out at West and began to "cross examine" the magistrate in disrespectful tones. Wood and West were once friends, but West's Catholicism and his political ties to Burton were anathema to Wood's new Klan clients—and perhaps to his own beliefs. West found Wood in contempt and fined him fifty dollars. Wood pledged to go to jail rather than pay the fine. He was saved from confinement when his son settled the bill.[70]

Puckett's arrest was not the Klan's biggest concern. The police department's secret investigation into the hooded order was at the root of Wood's anger. Mayor Burton denied approving the operation, but the Klan and its network inside municipal affairs "had a hunch" it was coming. Furthermore, Judge West's arresting party had been accompanied by at least one other observer that night, a keen reporter from the *Catholic Register*. The paper reported the results of its Klan investigation in the May 11, 1922 issue, furnishing its readers a list of "some men who may belong to the Klan." The *Register* explained that "we have sufficient evidence to lead us to believe and we are reasonably sure it was a meeting of the Klan, but as we do not believe in too much secrecy, we are printing below a list of men who we recognized leaving the hall." The names of more than ninety Klansmen appeared on the *Register*'s front page.[71]

The paper cleverly ridiculed the Klansmen's hypocrisy:

> *Klan members sign a pledge and take an oath to discriminate against the Negro, the Jew and the Catholic. They are not adverse, however, to taking these ostracized beings' money in a business way. For instance, there is Mr. Hartweg, who bought out the old Nelson Shoe Company on Central avenue. The present editor of the* Register *used to sell*

Mr. Hartweg advertising some thirteen years ago and Mr. Hartweg was profuse in his love for the Catholic, so he said. Probably someone else was using Mr. Hartweg's car and left it parked in front of Old Armory hall. That is up to Mr. Hartweg to prove to his Catholic customers.[72]

The *Register* promised to "make amends" if it incorrectly identified any of the men as Klansmen. One man quickly came forward and claimed that "knowing I am one of the Democratic candidates for office of sheriff…some have used this propaganda to injure me.…I wish to deny that I ever was or am now a member of said K.K.K." We do not know whether the *Register*'s editor believed T.A. Powell, but Powell's name appears on page one, column four, of a Kansas City Klan list stored at the Library of Congress. A former city councilman, Powell died in 1924. His pallbearers included Klansmen E.E. Stockdale and C.W. Peterson.[73]

The 1922 political season opened another battlefield in the Klan's war for Kansas City. Nineteen Klansmen entered the July primaries, seventeen as Republicans. Ten Klansmen moved on to the general election, where eight won office, including that of the county attorney. Four Klansmen sought the office of sheriff: Republicans David Kepler Jr. and Harry Lillich, and Democrats Powell and George Chess. Daniel "Bob" Maher, a non-Klan candidate, defeated Lillich by seventy-six votes. T.A. Flynn, a Catholic, won the Democratic nomination. Klansmen retreated to Paul Taneyhill's Armourdale drugstore to discuss their options.[74]

Judge West's harassment of the Klan had included fining a Lillich supporter, Edward Cooper, twenty-five dollars for displaying a placard too close to the primary polls. But the Klan blamed Lillich's defeat on vote fraud, not harassment. To circumvent their enemies, Klansmen decided to enter the grocer Lillich as an independent candidate. Bearing the signatures of "8,000 working men and their wives," a petition was submitted to the county requesting Lillich's name be placed on the November ballot. The bid met resistance, but County Attorney E.A. Enright, whose name also appears in Klan records, ruled Lillich eligible for the general election despite questions over the legality of some petition signatures.[75]

Lillich's reentry into the sheriff's race caused a shift in Kansas City politics, as Burton's allies deserted the Democrats for the Republican Maher to ensure the Klansman's defeat. Other anti-Klan forces also planned strategy. Five hundred members of the Retail Grocers Association, "equally divided in representation of colored, Catholic and Jew," backed Maher.[76] The race energized voters. Papers reported a 100 percent increase in Catholic registration. The *Kansas City (KS) Weekly Press* observed:

> On the other hand the Ku Klux Klan is very active and that organization… has been rolling up voters for the battle. Just what may be considered as the best test, is hard to determine. Flynn, Democrat nominee for sheriff, is a member of the Catholic church. Lillich who made the race for the Republican nomination for sheriff came out second best in the race…is said to be affiliated with the Klan.….Maher, who was nominated by the Republicans, is a member of the Presbyterian church and not a member of the klan. Many members of the Catholic church are said to believe that it's the part of wisdom to make a clean-cut campaign against the Ku Klux Klan and if that be true Maher may receive unexpected strength on that account.[77]

Maher got the Catholic, African American and Jewish boost he needed and won with 11,364 votes. Lillich finished second with 9,000, and Flynn was last with 7,046 votes. The anti-Klan strategy had succeeded for the time being, but 1922 marked only the beginning of Klan political action.[78]

Just as the *Catholic Register* warned when the Klan first appeared in Kansas City, the organization represented Burton's political enemies. Barely two months before the 1922 campaign, whispers of the kluxers' plans for the 1923 municipal elections began to appear in the news. "One such rumor," the *Kansan* reported, "said that an effort to raise $9,000 to finance the campaign of a Ku Klux Klan candidate would be made because of the fight Mayor Burton waged on the Klan when it first came into public notice here." Five prospective Klan candidates were mentioned for the mayor's race: Dr. R.B. Grimes, a non-Klansman backed by Klansmen N.V. Reichenecker and DeVirda H. Burcham; Klansman W.J. Wright Jr., former Wyandotte county sheriff; Klansman Dr. T.W. Hadley; G.B. Little, a non-Klan former city clerk; and William W. Gordon, a non-Klansman but brother of Klan member Dr. J. Riley Gordon. Burton finished first in the primary election with 8,503 votes, Gordon was second with 6,895 and Grimes a close third with 6,874 votes.[79]

Whether it said so on the ballot, the 1923 general municipal election would be a referendum on the Ku Klux Klan. Burton vowed to "continue to oppose strife and contention between the different groups in the city and I will, in the future as in the past, exercise a spirit of fairness in dealing with these problems." Burton's one mention of the Klan in his political advertisements referred to his opposition when the order first arrived in the city. Challenger

Gordon clearly directed his message to Klansmen and their fellow travelers. "The first thing I will do when I enter upon the duties of mayor will be to clean up Kansas City. It is my intention to thoroughly purge the city of bootleggers, gamblers, and other undesirable characters." Gordon defeated Burton by more than four thousand votes. "There are many causes assigned for the defeat of the mayor," the *Weekly Press* reported, "too numerous to mention." "One of which no doubt," the rival *Sun* rejoined, "was that the *Press* supported him."[80]

The Klan did its part by spreading rumors in African American neighborhoods that Burton had tried to join the hooded order. Klansman Harry Lillich claimed the mayor applied for Klan membership on December 21, 1921, but was rejected. (Coincidentally, this was the date of the Klan's first confirmed appearance in Kansas City newspapers.) Witnesses on the affidavit included Klansmen Vic Potter, N.V. Reichenecker, T.W. Hadley and William Hicks. Lillich's accusations appeared on the front page of the *Kansan* shortly after the election to add defamatory insult to the injury of Burton's loss. "It's all a dirty lie," Burton said. He sued Lillich for libel, but Judge Don C. McCombs, himself a member of No. 5, ruled that such cases with their $1,000 fines were out of his jurisdiction and dismissed the case.[81]

Viewing the influence of Catholic voters as alien to the interests of Kansas as the malignant *Kansas City Star*, Klansmen distributed bogus Knights of Columbus literature during the campaign. "This alleged oath is so revolting," Knights of Columbus state deputy James Malone said "that no self-respecting man will permit it be given to him, say nothing of distributing it to others." The outrageous sham oath warned voters of Catholic blood lust for the lives of Protestant babies, among other blood-chilling tales.[82]

The 1923 school board race also drew Klan candidates. What other assurance did Klan parents have of segregated pageants and jazz-free schools without control of the board? Four Klan candidates entered the contest for a two-year board term: George W. Durham, DeVirda H. Burcham, Bert R. Collins and Rosedale Klan No. 17 Exalted Cyclops Lawrence E. Wilson. (Rosedale became the city's eighth ward in 1922. It retained its separate Klan chapter, however.) Durham won a seat with 10,468 votes, followed closely by Burcham with 10,128 and Collins with 10,110. The similar vote totals illustrate the appeal of known KKK candidates beyond the klavern door, as Klan membership was less than half that number. The threesome's primary tallies were just as close. In the primary race for a four-year board term, Klansman Dr. K.C. Haas received 5,238 votes but faltered in the general municipal election.[83]

Mayor Gordon considered five Klansmen for chief of police: former sheriff W.J. Wright Jr., industrial security officer Clarence Hedrick, the ever-ready Harry Lillich and Kansas City police officers Stanley Beatty and U.G. Snyder. "At least four of the men in connection with the place would have difficulty in obtaining confirmation," the *Kansan* opined, "[and] presentation of their names would only result in embarrassment to them." Sensing the trouble a Klan nomination would bring, Gordon rewarded a non-Klan campaign worker, N.J. Wollard, with the post. Only one Klansman, Dr. Haas, was appointed to a position in the new administration. The medical man became the new police surgeon for the city's first district. But whatever disappointment the Klan suffered over Gordon's appointments, it had defeated Burton and also thereby eliminated Judge West from the police court bench and Chief Zimmer from the police force.[84]

On the face of it, it had been a good first year in the open for Wyandotte Klan No. 5. The hooded order's strength and influence was evident from the moment it entered Metropolitan Avenue Methodist Episcopal Church. Law enforcement, political power, moral probity, class and racial issues both defined the Klan's agenda and forced public debate. The ensuing war with Mayor Burton lasted from April 1922 to April 1923. The Klan won, but the order's first year in Kansas City was a limited success. As the city would soon learn, the Klan had suffered mightily at the hands of Burton, Judge West, the Catholic press and its own contradictions.

3

"METHODS AND OPERATIONS"

While Wyandotte Klan No. 5 offered a united front during the battles of 1922 and 1923, disagreement over "methods and operations" had sundered the chapter within months of receiving its official charter. The question of violence especially tested the resolve of Klansmen to impose their agenda on Kansas City and maintain their allegiance to the hooded order.

The trouble began in the early spring of 1922, when Exalted Cyclops DeVirda H. Burcham and Klabee Jesse H. Baxter traveled to Atlanta, Georgia, to "investigate conditions and learn something of the Klan and the organization" firsthand. What Burcham and Baxter did or did not learn in Georgia would be the main cause of the chapter's internal problems.[85]

As previously noted, Dr. Matthew E. Pearson, superintendent of Kansas City public schools, planned to integrate the city's spring school pageants by allowing African American and white children to march together in a parade. A mixed parade was intolerable to the Klan, but the appropriate course of action was yet to be determined.

Klan No. 5 had two branches subordinate to the exalted cyclops, whose identities were unknown to the klavern's general membership. The "Cabinet" provided the exalted cyclops with internal security and reviewed the complaints collected by the Klan. The Cabinet, also known as the "Klokann," comprised both chapter officers and others selected by Burcham. But the Cabinet was deliberative. A shadowy clandestine element dubbed the "kluxers" executed the order's direct actions. Burcham presented the Pearson matter to the Cabinet, where he allegedly proposed that the kluxers disguise themselves in special robes unmarked with Klan insignia, don masks and punish the superintendent for his affront to white supremacy.

Burcham's "night riding" order, according to Klansman Louis S. Harvey, was the real lesson brought back from Atlanta. Harvey said it was there that Burcham learned

> *how…* [to] *execute these orders of the cabinet and carry them into effect by taking people out and administering punishment; he* [Burcham] *said they were instructed how to disguise themselves so they would not be recognized and that was by stuffing cotton in their mouths or jaws.* [So] *that the punishment they administered was effective…they did not attempt to permanently maim a person or kill them, but just so they would know they had been dealt with by the Klan.*[86]

Harvey and fellow Cabinet members Richard R. Fleck, Cresse P. Rhoads and J.C. Hopkins balked at Burcham's plans. "I remember saying to them if there was anything wrong with the matter, we should take it up with Professor Pearson; so we called his house and made arrangements to see him that evening," Harvey said. In the end, Burcham led a contingent of unrobed Klansmen to the superintendent's house, where they peaceably and duly persuaded him to cancel the parade plan.[87]

Burcham had his own version of events. He maintained that the purpose of his Atlanta trip was to meet Imperial Wizard William Simmons, whose only instruction to the visitors was to "follow the constitution and by-laws" of the Klan. Burcham also denied the existence of the kluxers and their unmarked robes. He contended that the consideration of community complaints was not limited to the Cabinet but was referred to the regular membership. After the members gathered evidence, he said, he relayed the information to public officials. Burcham further stated that the Pearson problem was discussed during a regular membership meeting. But ten other Klansmen corroborated Harvey's charge, including Harry R. Borchardt, an admitted member of the kluxers; J.C. Hopkins, the member who ordered the manufacture of the plain kluxer robes; and Gerald Keith, the Klan tailor who made the garments. To add to the confusion, Dr. Pearson later denied the effect the visit had on his decision to cancel the parade, although one wonders if the statement was made in order to prevent a second visit by the Klan.[88]

The controversy ignited by Burcham and Baxter's Atlanta trip made it clear the Klan would not survive intact if its leaders advocated physical violence as a means to achieve its vision for the city. Louis S. Harvey, a former assistant U.S. attorney who had helped prosecute the Industrial Workers of the World in a celebrated trial related to the Red Scare (fear of left-wing infiltration and violence) after World War I, suspected that Burcham's alleged plans for Pearson were unlawful. He discovered that an "old statute put on the books after the Civil War had been carried forward into Section 19 of the federal statutes, which explained…that if two or more persons conspired to intimidate a person from exercising his rights, he was guilty of conspiracy and subject to federal punishment." Harvey concluded that Burcham's plan "would amount to a violation of the federal statutes, and I did not feel justified in letting the members go farther without apprising them of what their actions meant in the face of the law." At the next meeting of the Klan, on July 13, 1922, Wyandotte Klan No. 5 voted to "disband." On Harvey's advice, 450 men left the order in a single day.[89]

Conflict tore at the fabric of No. 5's future. Disagreements over chapter funds, particularly the "amount of money they wanted sent to Atlanta at that time," exacerbated the tension. Klansman V.A. Simons blamed the chapters' "bust up," in part, on the money issue. He did not elaborate on the details. But the *Catholic Register* boasted:

> So much trouble was caused the Klansmen through this publicity [the *Register*'s exposé of Klan members] that they got to fighting amongst themselves. Then Kleagle Jones saw that the end was near and ordered the treasurer to turn over the several thousand dollars in the treasury to him. The treasurer waxed so vehement in his refusal that he finally told Jones that "he would see him in hell fires before he would turn over a dime to him." Jones reported back to DeNise, and the King Kleagle had the Imperial gizzard revoke the charter of the Kansas City, Kas., Klan. The money is still on deposit in a Kansas bank.[90]

But the Klan did not revoke No. 5's charter until November, and only then to circumvent a state investigation of the order. Still, there is an element of truth to the *Register*'s claims. Burcham charged twenty-two Klansmen with attempting to "wreck" the order by the "appropriating of money and property." Although most of them quit in July, they were officially "banished" from the Klan on October 20, 1922. Among other Klan crimes, it was charged that J.C. Hopkins "had received money and issued receipts"

OFFICIAL DOCUMENT

TO ALL EXALTED CYCLOPS, TERRORS AND KLANSMEN, IN THE REALMS OF KANSAS AND MISSOURI, GREETINGS!

You are hereby officially advised that the following named men were banished by Wyandott Klan No.5, Realm of Kansas, for conduct unbecoming Klansmen, their banishment conforming in every respect to the Constitutional laws and requirements of our Order:

FLECK, R. R.	BAXTER, Jesse
HOPKINS, J. C.	HOPKINS, C. C.
RHODES, C, P.	CRUDEN, Dave
HADLEY, T. W.	BULLOCK, H. A.
JOHNSON, J. M.	BRENNER, H. P.
SIMMONS, V. A.	HARVEY, L. S.
LOWELL, C. C.	LUTZ, L. E.
LILLICH, Harry	BOYER, Lester
HADDEN, W. W.	WHITE, C. E.
CLARK, C. D.	TANEYHILL, Paul
DINGLE, Henry	DINGLE, Louie

Therefore, because these men have forfeited their rights to citizenship in the Invisible Empire, all Klansmen are enjoined under the provisions of their sacred oaths and the requirements of the Constitution of our Order from having any dealings or communications with them whatsoever pertaining to our fellowship.

Given under my hand and seal this the Twentieth day of the Tenth month of the Year of Our Lord, Nineteen Hundred and Twenty Two; and on the Dreadful day of the Weeping Week of the Mourning month of the Year of the Klan LVI.

IMPERIAL KLIGRAPP,
Knights of the Ku Klux Klan, Inc.

Twenty-two Klansmen were banished from No. 5 for organizing reform Klans or other unnamed offenses. *Kansas Historical Society.*

but failed to record the transactions in Klan account books. The charge was apparently retaliation against Hopkins for testifying that Burcham ordered him to buy the unmarked kluxer robes.[91]

The Invisible Empire had struggled with the violence issue as the Klan tried to outgrow its southern night-riding origins. Infamous Klan attacks in

Texas and Oklahoma led to a national coup of the organization by men who wanted to move into legitimate arenas of conflict, namely politics. Despite the new national leadership, the Klan would continue to wrestle with the violent image and its own violent acts and tendencies. This was the case in Kansas City throughout the twenties, especially after the exodus of some of the more reasonable men following the Pearson affair. Klan member Dr. T.W. Hadley testified during a state investigation of the Klan that while no "methods" were directly discussed for dealing with a local troublemaker, it was "something implied" that drove him from the order. Klansman D.H. Vance recalled a heated meeting over how to punish a wife deserter. The meeting "broke up in argument," but before the evening ended, "it was proposed…to go out and call on the man and tell him to get back to his wife." Vance did not elaborate on the methods used.[92]

Wyandotte Klan No. 5 had its share of violent men. Newspaper accounts preserve their brutish acts. Mrs. Thomas C. Hattley, for example, sued her Klan husband for divorce, charging that he was "an habitual drunkard, [and] that he has abused her and used vile language." Hattley was soon arrested for striking her with a pistol and public drunkenness. It was her fifth attempt at divorce.[93]

Despite the KKK's official commitment to enforcing the prohibition amendment, the Klan constitution permitted the drinking of alcoholic beverages except during chapter meetings. Beyond that, drinking was an offense only if judged to be "excessive" or "habitual," as in Hattley's case, although there is no evidence he was expelled from the Klan on that account.

In 1923, Hattley's perpetual drinking was blamed for the deadliest fire in Kansas City history, when apartments above his auto garage on the 900 block of Kansas Avenue burned due to his negligence. Thirteen tenants died, including a two-year old child. No charges were filed.[94]

Hattley's luck is perplexing. Years before the fire, he was in the dock for receiving stolen goods at his junk store but avoided jail. Hattley was later twice sentenced to alcohol treatment at the state sanitarium. He attacked his son with a knife following his discharge from yet another Missouri hospital, where he had taken the cure. The son responded by throwing his father from a running vehicle. Hattley senior was clearly a troubled man. And yet time after time, he was back in the news as a respected community leader, merchant and property owner. In a twisted headline, the paper described his new business venture, a post-fire restaurant, as a "Phoenix rising from the ashes." The *Press* also praised Hattley's "attractive" new filling station "where the garage destroyed by fire stood" as a benefit to the community.

No mention was made of the fire's victims. One must wonder what role the Klan may have played in preserving his reputation.[95]

Klansman Harry Lillich, who seemed always to be in some sort of scrape, was arrested for striking a journalist who attempted to photograph Klan members leaving a courtroom. "I didn't hit him," Lillich protested, then boasted, "if I had he wouldn't be here now." Judge West, who had already proven his hostility to the Klan, smacked Lillich with a $200 fine.[96]

William G. Bird, longtime county assessor, struck J.M. Crockett in the face when the accountant accused the Klansman of factoring his politics into property assessments. Bird told the *Kansan* he had "tried to be reasonable but Crockett's remarks were too insulting." The scuffle lasted several minutes. Bird's wounds were confined to his hands; Crockett nursed a bloody nose.[97]

Exalted Cyclops A.W. Murray, who took over the leadership of No. 5 in 1927, was accused of sending a "threatening and abusive letter" to Mrs. C.R Woodside—threatening just what, the papers did not say. Murray denied the charge. The Klan offered a $100 reward for the arrest and conviction of the writer. The money went unclaimed.

Klansmen claimed violent threats against themselves, too. No. 5 secretary C.W. Sayers was cooling down on his front porch late one summer night when he saw three men approaching with what he feared was a bomb. Sayers pulled a sidearm and fired three shots at the strangers, who escaped unscathed. Klansmen found dynamite near Sayers's home the next day. Round-the-clock guards stood post until the danger passed. Sayers blamed the attempted bombing on Klan efforts to clean up the city's liquor joints.[98]

Besides the acts of individual Klan members, the violence and threats of violence perpetrated by Wyandotte Klan No. 5 were dedicated to maintaining white supremacy. A growing issue vexing Klansmen was where to educate Mexican children as more Hispanic families arrived in Kansas City. To the great concern of white parents, Emerson School in the Argentine district accommodated more than one hundred Mexican children in its crowded classrooms. Neighborhood leader Dr. K.C. Haas of the Argentine Activities Association and the Ku Klux Klan, along with a representative of the Parent Teachers Association, approached the Mexican consulate in search of permission to build a separate school for the immigrant children. The official agreed, and the issue faded for a time thanks to the diplomacy of the Klansman and his colleague, the wife of a fellow Klan member. But other Klansmen, impatient with the building of a segregated school, invoked the violence option and clashed with Mexican residents over the school question. The affray is more evidence of the divide within the order over physical and more genteel types of Klan coercion.[99]

The Klan occasionally threatened white residents who failed to live up to their standards for the race—wife abusers, bootleggers, misguided school officials—but African Americans garnered the most Klan attention. George McClelland, who sold real estate to African Americans, received a warning letter from the Klan in June 1922. The threat read, "Warning!!! You are on the list for a tar and feathering on account of you and your agents locating colored tenants in white neighborhoods. Besides, your office will be dynamited. Look out for your life. K.K.K., PS This is no boy's play." Police dismissed the Klan connection because of the note's poor paper quality and the author's poor penmanship. But the police force included numerous Klansmen, most importantly, the department's day and night captains, U.G. Snyder and Stanley Beatty. McClelland, not wanting to get Klan sheets in a twist, theorized that the threat came from parties in the vicinity of Fourth and Fifth Streets and Greeley Avenue, where he had recently sold property to African Americans. McClelland, incidentally, is identified as "mulatto" in the 1920 census, a status that would have automatically made him suspect in Klan eyes.[100]

There was no doubt that Wyandotte Klan No. 5 nailed a "vacate" order to the home of Willis H. Summers at 549 Greeley, one of the homes sold by McClelland. Summers caught the one hundred Klansmen in the act. The father of five children confronted the mob on his own. The Klansmen ordered him to abandon his new home because it was located between two white families. They gave him until the next evening to move out. Summers led a delegation of ten African Americans to Captain Beatty to plead for police protection. Beatty said no and referred the men to the state attorney general. He promised to confer with local Klan leaders, however, an easy vow given his personal connection to the order. Summers stood his ground. A former schoolteacher and World War I veteran, Summers remained in his home until the 1940s.[101]

W.M. McDonald, an African American citizen residing at 1411 South Twentieth Street, received a threatening note signed "K.K.K." in April 1923. The *Kansan* opined, "The writer, no doubt, fearing to reveal his identity, sought to conceal himself beneath the cloak of the K.K.K. and thus accomplish his purpose, all of which lends substance to the argument that the K.K.K. is a menace because of that very cloak." Given the Klan's dedication to white supremacy, more African Americans were probably driven from their homes, or at least pressured to leave. The historian is at the mercy of the sources, however, which failed to report much of African American life or misfortunes, especially in the pages of the white press.[102]

The letters to McClelland, Summers and McDonald are authentic. But other writers, whether members of the Invisible Empire or not, used the Klan's cloak to intimidate public officials, just as former mayor Harry Burton warned they would when the hooded order first entered the city. Governor Jonathan Davis received numerous Klan or alleged Klan letters in his Topeka office, for example:

> *We See By the Papers that James McMahon sent up to Lansing in 1909 was asking for pardon from you. To Wich we Seriously Protest. We No the full facts in his case he murdered his Brotherinlaw and 2 Sisters in Cold Blood. Besides his married Sister was Ready to Be A Mother in Short Time So you See he practicable killed 4 Persons these are facts Knowed to all the Old Settlers hear So we don't want you to Ever Let him out to come back in Wyandotte county. if he is turned Loose in hear he Will Be Roped to a Limb of a tree. We are your Friends and ask you to Keep him Where he is Let Him Rot there for all We care. Trust you will see to it he dont come Back Hear. Fraternally the KUKlux Klan of. Wyandotte. Co. Kan.[103]*

Scrawled on cheap paper and lacking the organization's usual design mummery, the letter is clearly a fraud. Official Klan correspondence was generally sober, if officious, as in this case:

> *Honorable Jon. Davis, Governor of Kansas, Sir: It is with regret that we note your appointment of Harry B. Burton to a responsible position in the state prison at Lansing. And in as much as that Harry B. Burton has taken advantage of every opportunity to oppose our organization during his administration as Mayor of our city; thus compelling us to defeat him for reelection—We feel keenly disappointed to learn of him receiving an appointment to a position of responsibility by the Governor of our State who we have felt to be friendly to our cause. Therefore we most earnestly protest to you of this appointment and sincerely hope that you will take steps to amend this situation in the near future. Most sincerely yours, Wyandotte Klan No. 5, Knights of the Ku Klux Klan, John L. Zeller, Kligrapp, PO Box 117, Kansas City, Kansas.[104]*

Burton first accepted but then quickly declined the appointment.

"WYANDOTTE"

KLAN NUMBER 5 — REALM OF KANSAS

Knights of the Ku Klux Klan

KANSAS CITY, KANSAS

July 18, 1923.

Honorable Jon. Davis
Governor of Kansas.

Sir:

It is with regret that we note
your appointment of Harry B. Burton to a resposible
position in the state prison at Lansing.

And in as much that Harry B. Burton has taken
advantage of every opportunity to oppose our organization
during his administration as Mayor of our City; thus
compelling us to defeat him for reelection,— We feel
keenly disappointed to learn of him receiving an
appointment to a position of responsibility by the
Governor of our State whom we have felt to be friendly
to our cause.

Therefore we most earnestly protest to you
of this appointment and sincerely hope that you will
take steps to amend this situation in the near future.

Most sincerely yours,
Wyandotte Klan No. 5,
Knights of the Ku Klux Klan.

Kligrap

P.O.Box 117 Kansas City, Kansas.

PRINTED BY THE KU KLUX PRESS

Wyandotte Klan No. 5 opposed the appointment of former mayor Burton to a position at the state penitentiary. *Kansas Historical Society.*

The Klan also employed vandalism in its campaign to reassert the dominance of white, native-born Protestants in Kansas City. The news surfaced when M.R. Russell, president of the St. John's Cemetery Association, accused an organization claiming to promote "100 Percent Americanism" as responsible for desecrating Catholic tombstones. More than twenty stones had been overturned and destroyed. Mayor Gordon assigned a guard to the graveyard's gate to prevent further damage. "Despite the watch that has been kept," the *Kansan* noted, "additional tombstones have been reported as having been turned over or demolished." Police surmised that the vandals' success indicated "that the person or persons who are wrecking the monuments are doing so methodically and carefully." Unlike the living African American residents, the city's dead received police protection.[105]

Kansas City Klansmen did not limit themselves to physical violence in their campaign to conquer the city. There was more than one weapon in their arsenal, including the boycott. No. 5 boycotted non- or anti-Klan merchants to promote fraternalism with fellow members and punish enemies. Fraternalism, or "Klannishness," as defined by Imperial Kligrapp (national secretary) H.K. Ramsey, meant to "stick to your own kind in every way." Klan newspapers in Wichita and Kansas City, Missouri, featured buying guides to the Klan-owned businesses in their communities. The Missouri guide alone advertised the businesses of more than 350 Klansmen. Klannishness worked in the other direction, too. No. 5 encouraged its members to "refrain from buying" from a dry-goods merchant because he refused to advertise in a local newspaper. The paper was not identified, but the *Kansan* was the likely beneficiary of Klan action. Klansmen alleged that the *Kansas City Star* had ignored Kansas political affairs until the advent of a daily rival in Kansas, the *Kansan*, in 1920. Fearing the loss of advertising revenue, the *Star* began to report and, critics averred, direct Kansas politics. By mid-May 1922, the *Kansan* and *Star* were in an advertising war. Boycotting merchants who refused to advertise in the *Kansan* was consistent with both the Klan's anti-*Star* vendetta and its Klannishness. Although the *Kansan*'s editorial page was moderately anti-Klan, Klansmen held important positions at the paper, including in the advertising department.[106]

Elected Klan officials wielded state power in their battle for the city. This tactic is evident in the actions taken by Wyandotte County attorney Justus N. Baird when he began enforcing a neglected nineteenth-century statute barring Sunday labor and grocery sales. Buttressing the supremacy of white, native-born Protestant cultural norms thought to have been lost to mass immigration was part of the Klan's campaign to keep Kansas City "100 Percent American." Observers noted the "religion" (pro-Protestant) aspect of Baird's efforts from the beginning of his war on Sunday work in July 1923 when grocer Mike Schanker, of Russian Jewish background, protested that *his* Sabbath was on Saturday. Schanker assured Baird he observed the day by locking his shop up "tighter than a drum." Other grocers stayed open on the humanitarian grounds that many poor people did not have refrigerators. Meat and milk purchased on Saturday would spoil by Monday.[107]

The *Kansan* reported the controversy over the Sunday hours "as one of the biggest quarrels Kansas City has witnessed for some time." Baird assigned a special criminal investigator to survey law violators. The investigator reported that thirty-five stores remained open on the first Sunday of his reconnaissance. The next Sunday saw seventy stores defy the county attorney's enforcement of the 1868 law.[108]

The defiant grocers hired their own counsel and prepared for legal battle. Baird escalated the conflict by ordering the arrest of nearly twenty grocers; the next weekend, he arrested thirty more. The defendants' names give some evidence of the ethno-cultural tensions at the base of the conflict: Moskos, Callas, Siapaka, Ruskairck, Fitzpatrick and Stempleman. These are all names from countries and traditions that have not necessarily observed the Sabbath in the same manner as citizens of northern European Protestant descent, of the elite and mythical "Nordic" race of Klan belief. Further evidence of the tension is the fact that the names of County Attorney Baird and Assistant County Attorney J.W. Hayward are found on the membership roster of Wyandotte Klan No. 5. The special investigator had Klan ties as well.[109]

The grocer trials continued through the summer of 1923. The issue was finally settled in December when the case of grocer Dan O'Donnell was filed before the state supreme court "for the purpose of obtaining an expression of the court as to the intention of the statutes involved." O'Donnell won his appeal, and the Grocer War slipped from the news.[110]

The county attorney was not the only Klansman to use his official power to further Klan aims. The Reverend George W. Durham utilized his seat on the board of education to censor books in the public library. Durham seized all five copies of *Elmer Gantry* and locked them in the library vault. Durham disliked author Sinclair Lewis's depiction of Protestant clergymen in the novel. Although the Klan succeeded in sacking the Argentine High School dancing instructor in 1922, Durham led an annual campaign against dancing of any variety in city schools.[111]

If the internal battles over "methods and operations" had not been enough, Wyandotte Klan No. 5's problems were further compounded by Kansas governor Henry J. Allen's attacks on the order. Allen became aware of the Klan's presence in the state in late July 1921. Allen, like Mayor Burton, was concerned with the prospect of Klan growth, but the issue remained dormant until July 1, 1922, when 400,000 railroad shop workers went out on strike, 7,500 of whom were in the two Kansas Cities.[112]

Allen was acutely sensitive to labor unrest. Kansas endured more than three hundred coal strikes between 1917 and 1919 alone. In an attempt to curb the work stoppages, Allen called a special session of the legislature in January 1920 to establish the Court of Industrial Relations, better known as the "Industrial Court." The court regulated five "public interest" services, such as energy and transportation. The court could forbid work stoppages without its permission and set criteria for wages and working hours. But

Governor Henry J. Allen's stubborn opposition to the KKK prevented the hooded order from gaining legal recognition in the Sunflower State. *Kansas Historical Society.*

more important, "the [court] stated that [while] collective bargaining was upheld, it was unlawful to use the strike, boycott, picketing and intimidation for the purpose of hindering, delaying or interfering with or suspending the operation of an essential business." It was also unlawful to encourage a strike or strikers in print or speech.[113]

Labor hated Allen's court and sought redress. Opportunistic organizers presented the Klan as the solution. Eager recruits, workers themselves, donned the white robe and pledged to march in support of the strikers in Arkansas City, Kansas, on July 4, 1922. In the event, the parade was canceled, but on July 8, Allen announced that masked parades would be prohibited in Kansas. "Masks [were] an unhealthy condition while strikes were in progress," Allen said.[114]

The worried governor soon began exploring how to banish the KKK from the state altogether. Allen determined the Klan was operating in Kansas without a corporate charter; in other words, "no [legal] authority to enter Kansas has been granted to the Klan." Nevertheless, the order kept growing. Newspapers from the summer of 1922 are flush with reports of Klan recruiting success from Kansas City to the Colorado state line. At the end of September, Allen dispatched undercover agents to investigate conditions in Arkansas City, the site of continuing Klan and labor strife. The investigation evolved into a larger examination of the Invisible Empire in Kansas.[115]

As the tension between Allen and the hooded order grew, the governor decided to address the issue in Coffeyville, Kansas, a citadel of Klan strength. Allen left on the trip amid threats to himself and his family. The governor reportedly "had no fixed opinions as to whether the messages came from a supporter of the Klan or from a radical labor representative who sought to use the Klan to carry out a cowardly plan of intimidation." But if the governor knew who his enemies were, he did not seem to realize that the Klansman and the labor radical might be the same man.[116]

Though perhaps not a radical, the Reverend George Durham cheered organized labor mightily from his pulpit and other platforms. "Under the industrial court law of this state, I am violating its rulings by telling you I am in sympathy with the strikers," Durham confessed to an audience of workers. But "a laboring man cannot support a family and educate his children to be a credit to the republic under the new [wage] scale," Durham said to the huzzahs of a thousand strikers.[117]

In Coffeyville, Allen denounced the Klan as "the greatest curse that can come to any civilized people, the curse that arises out of unrestrained passions of men governed by religious intolerance and racial hatred." Allen threatened to oust the Klan from Kansas on the grounds that it was a foreign corporation (Atlanta, Georgia) operating in the state without permission of the state charter board. He accused the order of "seeking to establish in this state the un-American idea that we can improve the conditions of this state by turning the rights of government over to a masked organization which arrogated unto itself the right to regulate the individual."[118]

Allen continued the crusade in Great Bend, Kansas. "My objection to the Klan is not on account of any particular principle," he admitted. "My objection is to its masked form of government." Then Allen, doing what politicians do best, turned around and pointed his attack toward the Klan's most reviled enemy, Roman Catholics. Like many of the Klansmen he opposed, Allen was a Methodist and a Mason. He also subscribed to the same anti-Catholic myths. "Bloc voting" and undermining public schools, the "cornerstone of the republic," were common anti-Roman complaints. "You Catholics who go out and say, 'I don't vote for a man that is not Catholic. I am going to put my political activities behind my religion.' You ought to be ashamed of yourselves," Allen said. "I know that the Catholic church has been guilty of some unwise duties toward the school system because there should be in this country, as the basis of our citizenship, the English language." While Allen opposed the Klan, he could also count. He and his Republican party had more Klan votes to lose than Roman Catholic votes, thus his self-abasement.[119]

Following a summer and fall of investigation, Kansas attorney general Richard J. Hopkins filed a suit on November 21, 1922, seeking to oust the Klan from the state. The state also secured a list of Kansas City Klan members collected by federal agents in an aborted national investigation of the hooded order. On April 30, 1923, Hopkins's men began hearing the testimony of Kansas City men named on the list. The *Kansan* reported six African American men present to observe the proceedings. Press coverage of the investigation exposed the Klan's intimidation of school superintendent Matthew E. Pearson and the firing of the dancing instructor at Argentine High School, as well as the inner workings of the order. The articles divulged the Klan's dissension and the July 13, 1922 breakup. The stories included the names of more than forty Wyandotte Klan No. 5 members, surely an embarrassment to the men and their families.[120]

So, despite the Klan's victorious appearance in the wake of Mayor Burton's defeat in the city elections, the order was divided and exposed by the end of April 1923. Internal strife, the official pressure applied by Mayor Burton and Governor Allen, combined with the hounding by the *Catholic Register*, had forced the Klan to defend and examine itself. Upon examination, scores of members left.

The men who walked out of the Klan between July 1922 and May 1923, however, were not abandoning their Klan hopes or ideals. "The whole thing, methods and operations, have become so distasteful to me I don't want to think about it," one disgusted Klansman said. Then he did what any concerned citizen would do.[121]

He organized.

4
REFORM AND REACTION

PART I: A TENDENCY TO SPLIT

Desertion from the ranks of Wyandotte Klan No. 5 had started even before the July 13, 1922 "bust up," when a challenger appeared in Kansas City to compete with the Klan for the allegiance of white Protestant activists. Led by rebel Klansmen Cresse P. Rhoads, V.A. Simons, Richard R. Fleck, Bert R. Collins, L.F. Lutz, F.B. Croll, J.C. Hopkins, W.H. Williams, Paul Taneyhill, O.S. Clark and C.E. White, the "Knights of America" formed on July 6. "We couldn't longer control the klan organization, so we killed it and organized a new anti-Catholic society to fight Catholics and Jews only. We will let Negroes join this society as most of our members like Negroes anyway and they ought to be a big help to us in the new organization," said an ex-Klansmen to the *Catholic Register*.[122]

A prospective Knight was at least eighteen years old, male, Protestant and, notwithstanding the *Register*, white. The Knights' principles of "Loyal Americanism, Protestant Christianity, and white supremacy" were nothing more than a litany of standard Klanisms. Probably as reflective of the worries that led men to organize the Knights is the statement of Reverend N.V. Tatum on the occasion of the group's founding. "It is high time," Tatum said, "that the common people are making some effort to organize against crooked political and criminal influences. Labor is organized, capital is organized, the underworld, politicians; in fact, everyone except common people are organized," Tatum proclaimed. "We must organize with the intent to act unitedly in the common cause of the common people." Like the Klan, the Knights of America offered Kansas Citians of the right stripe a collective way to organize their discontent.[123]

Three hundred men joined the Knights at the inaugural meeting held at Tatum's Welborn Community Church. Klansman E.A. Enright, Wyandotte county attorney, was among those attending the convention. Although the Knights received a charter to operate legally in the state, the organization faded quickly. By November 1922, the Knights' biweekly meeting notices had disappeared from the newspaper. But disgruntled white Protestant hopes died hard, and the Knights' founders and members soon reappeared in both the Atlanta-based Klan and subsequent local Klan organizations.

On May 1, 1923, the "Ku Klux Klan of Kansas" became the second Kansas City reform Klan to file a charter application in Kansas. Led by former No. 5 members Harlan A. Bullock, J.C. Hopkins, L.F. Lutz, F.B. Croll and Claude F. Higgins, the Kansas Klan was the result of the ouster suit investigation initiated by Governor Henry J. Allen. Removing the "objectionable features" opposed by state leaders, "the new Klan will recognize no boycott, no class hatred and will not wear masks or hooded uniforms," explained the group's attorney, Louis S. Harvey.[124]

This reformed Klan was tailored to fit the specific objections of Governor Allen in the fall of 1922, when he made clear that his opposition to the Klan was not based on any "particular principle." "The essence of our opposition to this order," Allen said, "is not in the fact that it fights the Catholic church or expresses its antipathy to the Jews or to the Negro, but in the fact that it does this under the protection of a mask and thru process of terrorism and violence."[125]

Allen explained that he did not fear the Catholic Knights of Columbus, because he knew who the state leaders were. He could not say the same of the Klan. Any successful reformed Klan would have to allay establishment fears of its secret leadership and threats to its monopoly on violence.

Following the example of the Knights of America, the "Preamble" to the "Constitution and Laws of the Knights of the Ku Klux Klan" (Kansas) was a simple adaptation of select principles from the Atlanta Klan's constitution. But there were several important omissions. The Kansans dropped the residual "southerness" of the Atlanta organization. References to chivalry and the protection of womanhood (with its racist undertones of miscegenation) were dropped from the document. The Kansans made other changes to the Atlanta Klan constitution to improve its acceptability to outsiders. Whereas the Imperial Wizard reserved all power in the autocratic Georgia order, the "government of the [Kansas Klan] shall be patterned after the constitution of the United States of America, and shall be ever democratic in form." The local reformers promised executive, legislative and judicial branches "substantially the same as the federal government." The local units envisioned by the Kansans would manage their own finances and write and enact their own constitution for the "absolute government of themselves." The Kansans also eliminated the occult officer titles (wizards, cyclops, titans) favored by the Atlanta Klan and used military ranks instead.[126]

The Kansas Klan required its members to be "Protestant Gentiles" and American citizens. This expanded, however slightly, the Atlanta Klan's definition of an American, which was limited (officially, at least) to native-born white men. Section five of the Kansas constitution addressed the state's fear of the Klan's secrecy. "The membership and roster of this organization shall not be any more secret than is the membership of any other fraternal, benevolent organization or secret society in the United States of America," the reformers pledged. Furthermore, the Kansas Klan assured the state that no member would be "required or permitted to wear a mask over his face or to otherwise conceal his identity" in public. Confident that the reforms would prove acceptable to the state charter board, the Ku Klux Klan of Kansas submitted its application for admittance, only to wait for an approval that would never come.[127]

The tendency of Klan chapters to split up, regroup and reform in order to retain members and gain legality is a national characteristic of the KKK in the 1920s. Disgruntled Denver, Colorado Klansmen, among numerous examples, formed the Minute Men of America. The new order, writes historian Robert Goldberg, "abandoned the more controversial features… of the Invisible Empire while retaining the Klan's concern with law, order, morality, the separation of church and state, and immigration." The Minute Men, and Women, attempted organization in Kansas in 1925, but they never completed their charter application.[128]

Muncie, Indiana, perhaps better known as the archetypal "Middletown" of a famed sociological study, suffered the same calamitous fissures as Kansas City. Organized in March 1924 as the "Klan of the North," the Muncie-based order had national ambitions. It soon appeared in Kansas as the "Independent Klan of America." This new take on the hooded order applied for a charter to operate in Kansas in early 1925 but was rejected by the state charter board on May 7 unanimously and without explanation. Threatened with a lawsuit for their unauthorized use of the

Application for Authority to Engage in Business in the State of Kansas as a Foreign Corporation.

TO THE CHARTER BOARD OF THE STATE OF KANSAS:

The_____ THE MINUTE MEN OF AMERICA _____, a corporation

organized under the laws of the State of_____ COLORADO _____, applies for permission to engage in

business in the State of Kansas, and for that purpose submits the following statement, to wit:

FIRST.

A certified copy of its Charter or Articles of Incorporation, which is filed herewith.

SECOND.

The place where the principal office or place of business of said corporation is located is_____

_____DENVER, COLORADO_____

THIRD.

The place where the principal office or place of business in this State is to be located is_____

_____TOPEKA, KANSAS_____

FOURTH.

The full nature and character of the business in which said corporation proposes to engage within the State

of Kansas is for the purpose of organizing a body of citizens pledged to unitedly
serve and defend our country and its constitutions and laws, to cultivate
the worship of God and the practice of the Christian religion, to maintain
law and order, to protect our pure womanhood, to promote charity, to establish just laws, to support the sovereignty of states' rights, freedom of
speech and press, separation of church and state, a closer relation between
capital and labor, limitation of foreign immigration, to effect wholesome
state, national and world legislation and reforms; to establish such local
organizations throughout the State of Colorado and elsewhere as may be deemed
advisable and beneficial; to acquire, own, possess, encumber and dispose of
real estate and personal property, to borrow money and secure the same upon
the property of the corporation, to transact its general business and to do
all other acts and things necessary and incidental to carrying out the
purposes of the corporation.

Dissident ex-Klansmen and women organized "reform" Klans. The Minute Men of America submitted its application for a state charter but never completed the process. *Kansas Historical Society*.

word "Klan," the hapless reformers renamed their sect the "Knights of American Protestantism." It promptly died.[129]

Former Kansas City Klansmen attempted reform once again in August 1924. These men also purged the order of its undemocratic features and secrecy, even going so far as to declare itself the "*Visible* Empire." Like its reformist predecessors, the Visible Empire also rewrote the constitution of Klan founder Simmons to remove the last vestiges of the KKK's distinctive southerness. Also like its reformist predecessors, the Visible Empire soon faded to literal invisibility.[130]

Kansas City reform Klansmen eliminated the order's masks, unveiled its membership, revolutionized its internal power structure, localized finances, dropped the order's southern accent and liberalized membership rules. But the Klan's most "objectionable feature" was its claim to a role in the affairs of state. This assertion was an offense to elected leaders that no amount of reform could ever make politically acceptable.

Part II: The Persistence of Anti-Catholicism

I am not against your organization because you don't like the Catholic church.
—*Governor Henry J. Allen, October 30, 1922*[131]

One change never considered by reform Kansas Klansmen was their attitude toward the Roman Catholic Church. There is a simple explanation for their retention of the Atlanta-based order's odious and vocal contempt of Rome. The Church was never included by friend or foe in the state as among the Klan's "objectionable features."

Catholic leaders saw right through the flimsy reforms of the dissident kluxers. "From the daily papers I learn that the new Klan is to be organized in Kansas City, Kansas, intends to discard the mask and other obnoxious features of the old Klan, doing this probably to comply with the regulations in obtaining a charter," wrote Bishop Augustus John Schwertner of Wichita to Knights of Columbus state deputy James Malone. "The new klan will probably be as anti-Catholic as the old Klan. With the mask removed they will more nearly resemble some of the protestant sects and secret societies, and probably become more openly identified with them in the future." Catholics knew "reform" Klansmen had no reason to change, nor would they see any profit in doing so.[132]

Diocese of Wichita
Chancery Office
Wichita, Kansas

May 9th 1923

Mr James Malone.
210 Crawford Bldg.
Topeka, Kansas.

My dear Mr Malone:-

Replying to your letter of May 5th asking for an opinion on the contents of the proposed letter to Bishop Ward regarding the granting of a charter to the New Klu Klux Klan, I beg to say that there are, no doubt, certain conditions required by the State of Kansas before any charter can be granted. If this new Klan complies with these prescribed conditions, I feel it would be difficult to induce the members of the State Charter Board to refuse a charter. From the daily papers I learn that the new Klan to be organized in Kansas City, Kansas, intends to discard the mask and some other obnoxious features of the old Klan, doing this probably to comply with the regulations in obtaining a charter. The new Klan will probably be as anti-Catholic as the old Klan. With the mask removed they will more nearly resemble some of the protestant sects and secret societies, and probably become more openly identified with them in the future.

There can be no doubt that a secret anti-Catholic propaganda is under way against the parochial schools and our other rights as Catholic citizens. To cope with

2.

this situation we need a well organized and wide awake laity back of our clergy. We must see that literature reaches non-Catholics, who are being misinformed and that the lies and slanders of the bigots are refuted in press and pamphlet. The literature of the N.C.W.C ought to be broadcasted all over the country.

The "ex-nun " lectures in our state are another evidence of their bigotry and hatred. The methods used at Great Bend are usually most satisfactory. Pratt is trying to counteract the evils of these lectures by a general distribution of Catholic literature. I hope other places will do likewise.

I wish to thank you for the prompt and complete account of the unfortunate occurence at the initiation at Ellinwood. If the parties in question fail to comply with their written promises I will notify you and expect the authorities of the Knights of Columbus to take the proper action for the good of the order and that particular council.

Very sincerely yours in Xto.

Hugh J. Schwertner
Bishop of Wichita.

Bishop Schwertner of Wichita expressed his concern over the lingering anti-Catholicism of the "reform" Klans. *Kansas Historical Society*.

The roots of American anti-Catholicism go back to the country's founding era. Historian John Higham writes that the "idea that papal minions posed a subversive threat to national freedom was so deeply entrenched in myth and memory that it needed little objective confirmation." Anti-Klan anti-Catholicism is a case in point. James Malone protested Governor Allen's October 1922 accusation of Catholic "bloc voting" and "unwise duties toward the public school." Malone said, "The quoted statement, 'Catholics who go out and say, "I do not vote for a man who is not a Catholic,"' is manifestly unfair to Catholics. Catholics never say, 'I do not vote for a man who is not a Catholic,' though many do not vote precisely because they are Catholics." In reply, Allen merely reiterated that the "Catholic who boycotted in election a man because he was not a Catholic is just as far away from the ideals of the American Republic as the Klansman who boycotted the man because he was a Catholic. This is religious bigotry, and has no place in our American life. And bigotry is just as bad for a Catholic as a Protestant."[133]

Allen viewed the Ku Klux Klan, an organization dedicated to his removal yet possibly a source of votes, and the Roman Catholic Church as moral equivalents. He found both groups narrow-minded, strident and unreasonable. Some opinion leaders shared Allen's view. "There is considerable satisfaction in the thought that John W. Davis [the 1924 Democratic presidential candidate] has been unable to drive President Coolidge to denouncing the Klan," remarked the *Kansas City (KS) Weekly Press*. "What kind of president would he be to denounce the Klan or the Knights of Columbus?"[134]

Protestant suspicion of Catholics was evident at nearly every level of the culture during the time of the Klan. Like County Attorney Justus N. Baird's use of an antiquated nineteenth-century law to enforce the Protestant Sabbath, the Kansas State Board of Review weighed its power to ban the 1924 "purely Catholic" film *White Sister*. Gertrude A. Sawtelle, a resident of Kansas City and chair of the review board, explained to Governor Jonathan M. Davis that while "there was nothing immoral or objectionable in the picture…we thought at the time it would only appeal to Catholics." On a similar note, Protestants in Ellsworth, Kansas, complained that the funeral services conducted by a Father Daniel M. Reidy for Catholic war dead returning from World War I were "too Catholic."[135]

Kansas had welcomed organized anti-Catholicism well before the Klan came to town. The American Protective Association (APA) thrived in Kansas City Protestant fraternal quarters, white and African American, from 1892 to 1897. The order's newspaper, the *American Eagle*, flourished during the APA's rise. The *Kansas City (KS) Gazette* rivaled the *Eagle* in its hatred of the Church, promoting anti-Catholic speakers, often "escaped nuns" whose tales offered pornographic depictions of religious life. The lurid tales of priests and nuns, and priests and priests, and nuns and nuns, and babies buried behind the convent caused some of their bearers to be imprisoned.

The "escaped nun" genre rose to prominence in the mid-1830s with the publication of two bestsellers detailing their heroines' getaway from Catholic captivity. Rebecca Reed's *Six Months in a Convent* and Maria Monk's *Awful Disclosures of the Hotel Dieu Nunnery* found an audience in a young, predominately Protestant country troubled by the immigration of Irish Catholics. Reed's book inspired the arson of the very Ursuline Convent where she once lived. Monk's credibility and book sales fell when it was discovered that she was not a former nun but rather a former prostitute.[136]

Reed's and Monk's picaresque escapes echoed in the pages of the *Gazette* as it championed the release of Annie Devers from the House of the Good

Shepherd by the Women's American Protective Association (WAPA). The Congregation of Our Lady of Charity of the Good Shepherd operated the house for the "reformation of young girls who either have fallen from virtue or whose incorrigible and immoral lives point to their speedy fall as certain." Among other wards, the house cared for prostitutes as young as twelve years old fleeing sexual slavery in the city's rough river bottom haunts. City courts assigned the girls to the sisters because the city lacked its own resources. Girls were released when they became of age.[137]

While the precise details of Annie Devers's case are unknown, her release is not. Mrs. J.W. Hile and Mrs. Winchester Rees of the WAPA secured Devers's discharge with a court order on the grounds that she was being held against her will. The women also demanded the freedom of twenty other women, all of whom were in danger of being returned to the very conditions that put them in the House of the Good Shepherd in the first place. The *Gazette* used the controversy to call for more public scrutiny of Catholic charitable organizations, as well as the elimination of parochial schools because of Devers's alleged illiteracy.[138]

The "escaped nun" story tradition continued into the Klan age. "Sister Mary Ethel" toured the Kansas City area in the 1920s with Invisible Empire support. Her talks on "Priests' Happy Hunting Grounds" and "The Veil, The Vows, My Escape" offered tales of women ruined in the convent to a new generation of wide-eyed Protestants.[139]

The APA's influence in Kansas City climaxed with the election of Mayor Nat Barnes, a member of the order, in 1894. Barnes's tenure featured the exclusion of Catholic children from the city's annual Decoration Day parade, an act presaging the Klan's attack on Dr. Pearson's integrated school pageant. State Labor Commissioner William G. Bird boosted his fellow APA man Barnes for governor in 1896 over the governor who appointed him commissioner. Bird would migrate to the Klan in the twenties.[140]

A few years after the APA's moment, an anti-Catholic movement emerged from the left of the political spectrum. "Progressive" anti-Catholicism linked big business with the Roman hierarchy. In March 1914, the *Iola (KS) Anti-Catholic Crusader* expressed the fears of nervous Kansas Protestants in this era. The *Crusader* explained to its readers "how the Jesuit political machine handles the bank....This is not a theory, but a condition. This is not a generalization, but a brass tack fact."[141]

In 1911, the *Menace*, a new "progressive" weekly anti-Catholic newspaper published in Aurora, Missouri, soon counted more than one million subscribers. The *Menace* aggressively pushed the entire repertoire of anti-

FREE PRESS, FREE SPEECH, FREE SCHOOLS, FREE STATE.

"Flag of the free heart's only home,
By Angel hands to valor given,
Thy Stars have lit the welkin dome
And all thy hues were born in
Heaven."

While we go to press, the Nation is covering the graves of the patriotic dead—a beautiful and grateful sentiment.

But to perserve and perpetuate free institutions for present and future generations requires a high order of faith, a bravery that enables a man to stand guard alone the darkest night, and a courage that glorifies the martyrs who die to make men free.

The MENACE defies the attempt of organized political Rome to destroy it.

A free press is the chief cornerstone of this government. The men are traitors, who, cloaked with a religious garb, with false lips praise the flag and stab the color guard in the back.

Buglers of freedom, sound the alarm! Beat the long roll!

Defenders of the flag and the foundations of government rally to the standard and do your duty.

—From the Menace of June 7, 1913.

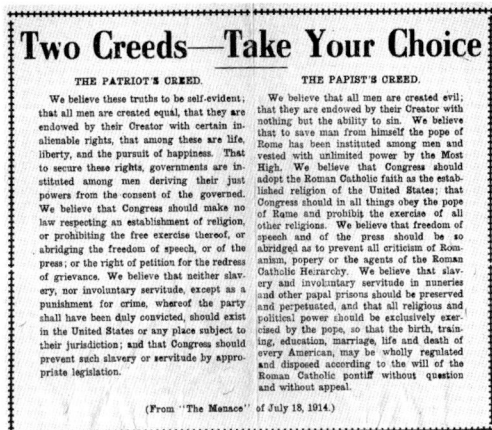

Two Creeds—Take Your Choice

THE PATRIOT'S CREED.

We believe these truths to be self-evident; that all men are created equal, that they are endowed by their Creator with certain inalienable rights, that among these are life, liberty, and the pursuit of happiness. That to secure these rights, governments are instituted among men deriving their just powers from the consent of the governed. We believe that Congress should make no law respecting an establishment of religion, or prohibiting the free exercise thereof, or abridging the freedom of speech, or of the press; or the right of petition for the redress of grievance. We believe that neither slavery, nor involuntary servitude, except as a punishment for crime, whereof the party shall have been duly convicted, should exist in the United States or any place subject to their jurisdiction; and that Congress should prevent such slavery or servitude by appropriate legislation.

THE PAPIST'S CREED.

We believe that all men are created evil; that they are endowed by their Creator with nothing but the ability to sin. We believe that to save man from himself the pope of Rome has been instituted among men and vested with unlimited power by the Most High. We believe that Congress should adopt the Roman Catholic faith as the established religion of the United States; that Congress should in all things obey the pope of Rome and prohibit the exercise of all other religions. We believe that freedom of speech and of the press should be so abridged as to prevent all criticism of Romanism, popery or the agents of the Roman Catholic Heirarchy. We believe that slavery and involuntary servitude in nuneries and other papal prisons should be preserved and perpetuated, and that all religious and political power should be exclusively exercised by the pope, so that the birth, training, education, marriage, life and death of every American, may be wholly regulated and disposed according to the will of the Roman Catholic pontiff without question and without appeal.

(From "The Menace" of July 18, 1914.)

Above: Anti-Catholic propaganda forced readers to make a stark decision. *Author's collection.*

Left: The anti-Catholic *Menace* magazine stoked the fires of anti-Romanism in the years between the demise of the American Protective Association and the rise of the second Ku Klux Klan. *Author's collection.*

Roman tropes of sybaritic priests, captive nuns and the bogus Knights of Columbus oath. The *Menace* also challenged the historicity of Christopher Columbus's "discovery" of America, submitting rather that the Chinese reached North American shores years before the Catholic Europeans.[142]

The "progressive" anti-Catholic movement was superseded by the Great War, but the zealous "100 Percent Americanism" born in the conflict's aftermath once again raised doubts of Catholic loyalty. Kansas City Catholics anticipated the possibility of postwar reaction. "During the past few weeks we have heard from several authorities that we may look for a drive against Rome in the near future," the *Catholic Register* reported in the spring of 1920. "There is need for Catholic action. We must have a crystallized Catholic sentiment," the paper warned. Within a year, their fears were realized as Klan kleagles arrived in the city to reawaken the latent anti-Catholicism.[143]

Under the leadership of Imperial Wizard Hiram Wesley Evans, the anti-Catholicism of the new Klan took on a more racist tone than previous anti-Papist outbreaks. Evans bought into the discussion taxonomies of Scientific

Racism, a pseudoscience inspired by Darwinian evolution that rated human populations by intelligence, accomplishments and entitlements. At the top of the scale reigned Nordics, people of northwestern European origins. Evans said the Klan represented "old stock pioneers" of the Nordic race, "the race which, with all its faults, has given the world almost the whole of modern civilization." Furthermore, the "old stock pioneers" of American settlement represented a refined branch of the Nordic race, one hardened and annealed by the frontier, which had brought its breeding up to new heights, "probably the highest in history." Nordics were anti-Catholic by nature, Evans averred. "The Nordic race is…almost entirely Protestant, and there remains in its mental heritage, an anti-Catholic attitude based on lack of sympathy with the Catholic psychology, on the historic opposition of the Roman Church to the Nordics' struggle for freedom and achievement, and on the memories of persecution." Kansas Grand Dragon (state president) Charles McBrayer "hated Catholics with a passion," his son told the author, "because his family was driven out of Scotland and Ireland by them." Similar unsubstantiated folk memories of persecuted French, German or English ancestors led legions of Kansas Citians into the Klan.[144]

Despite its natural superiority, the great Nordic race was foundering, Evans warned. Nordic complacency had invited strangers to take over their cities, their economy, their government. Aliens voted in blocs. Aliens refused to learn English. Aliens overbred. Aliens were constitutionally incapable of learning Americanism. Representing all that Evans and his Nordic nation despised in the alien was found in the Catholic Church and its autocratic Pope, the anti-Christ of alienism.[145]

Klan anti-Catholicism was directed at the "sub-races" of Caucasian Catholic immigrants from central, southern and southeastern Europe. Bohemians, Italians, Croatians—or "Alpines" and "Mediterraneans," in the nomenclature of the apostles of the new racism—were not quite white. The Klan's vow to the "eternal maintenance of white supremacy" was aimed not only at African Americans or Mexicans but also toward whites of inferior breeding.[146]

A Protestant view of the eternally alien Catholic is documented in a Klan newsletter by "M.H.S.," a Salina, Kansas woman:

A Methodist minister in this city made the statement that in the past year in 7 states the Methodists thought they were doing good work in caring for 3,000 orphans. It has been revealed that in the same 7 states 21,000 children had been taken in and cared for by the Roman Catholics. 21,000 deprived of the education of the free public school. It means the loss of 21,000 becoming American citizens; 21,000 more Roman Catholics. This is nothing short of a crime on the part of Protestant people.[147]

Kansas Governor Ben S. Paulen received numerous anti-Catholic missives in the Nordic supremacist campaign to keep the country comprehensively white:

January 30, 1925. Hon. B.S. Paulen. Topeka, KS. My Dear Governor, I am writing to advise you of some friction that exists among the State Board of Nurses. A Miss M. Helena Hailey R.N. Sec'y-Treas of State Board for Examination and Registrations of nurses is objectionable to some of the Board and I thought it advisable, owing to existing circumstances for you to give it due consideration. I am told by good authority that she is not fair. Also while nursing in a protestant hospital she took a child to care for, "which was a commendable thing to do," but since joining the Catholic Church is training it in this faith. I am enclosing news paper clipping to verify this statement. Now as Miss Hailey's place on the Board will be vacated with others this year, I would earnestly ask that a protestant be put on in her stead. I will give you two names of Nurses who are such and highly respected among their profession. Miss Bertha Pace of Clay Center and Mrs. C.C. Bailey 741 Tyler of Topeka KS, or any other protestant who is efficient should be acceptable to the remainder of the Board. I would not have you infer that I am trying to dictate who you shall appoint, am only asking that you do not reappoint this party, and that the ones you do appoint will be protestants. The Catholic are not entitled to an appointment from you, as none of them helped to elect you. I do not know if you remember me or not. You were meeting so many but I am the Dentist who got you to go to Bethany Hospital. I would much rather talk this over with you than write, and will not expect an answer from you, as you should be careful what you write. I will deem this as personal. I am yours truly. C.P. Rhoads.[148]

Dr. Rhoads, "banished" Klansman and Knights of America "Supreme Concillor," expressed sentiments typical of the pervasive anti-Catholicism that survived the several Klan reformation attempts.

No. 5's sister Klan in Arkansas City, Kansas, Klan No. 3, expressed its concern with the presence of Catholic teachers in public schools in a letter to Superintendent C.E. St. John. "You may be surprised and a little alarmed to received a communication from this order, but it is not our intention to

"ARKANSAS CITY"

Klan Number 3

Realm of Kansas

Knights of the Ku Klux Klan

ARKANSAS CITY, KANSAS

Sept- 8th-1922

Mr C. E. St John
Supt Of Public Schools
420 No 2nd St.
Arkansas City, Kansas.

Dear Sir:- We understand your situation, but as a body of
REAL RED BLOODED MEN, are for you and behind you in your
work.

You may be surprised and a little alarmed to
receive a communication from this order, but it is not
our intention to alarm you, but to call your attention
to a matter that we think requires attention.

We refer to the teachers in our Public Schools
who are Catholics, please read the letter we are enclose-
ing that we received, while we do not think much of the
letter without its signature, but this same question has
been before our body for some time, and no doubt you have
thought of this and may have been influenced to employ
these teachers who are of the Catholic faith, and had no
one to back you, now if this is the case you can rest
assure we will stand behind you in any thing you may do
to keep the influence of the Pope of Rome and his doctr-
ine away from our Children, and Schools.

While it is probably to late this year to do
much, but this should be keep in mind from now on and
you being a Mason and a Knight Templer, can see that our
Schools of Arkansas City be 100% PROTESTANT TEACHERS,
other towns and Cities are doing this , why not Arkansas
City?

YOURS FOR 100%.

KNIGHTS OF THE KU KLUX KLAN,

NO 3   Realm of Kansas.

PRINTED BY THE KU KLUX PRESS

The Klan threatened native-born white Protestants who failed to support its agenda. *Kansas Historical Society*.

alarm you, but to call your attention to a matter we think requires your attention." The Klan assured Mr. St. John that if he ever felt pressured to hire Catholics again, the KKK would have his back.

> *"We will stand behind you in anything you may do to keep the influence of the Pope of Rome and his doctrines away from our Children, and Schools," the Klan said. "While it is probably too late this year to do much, but this should be kept in mind from now on and you being a Mason and a Knights Templar, can see that our Schools of Arkansas City be 100% PROTESTANT TEACHERS, other towns and Cities are doing this, why not Arkansas City?"*

Examples like this abounded across Kansas in the 1920s.[149]

Propaganda distribution accompanied the letter-writing activities. "It is said something like 75 or 80 percent of the public offices in the United States are held or controlled by a secret organization known as the Knights of Columbus, whereas only about one-fifth of the voters of the country belong to this organization....Is this true?' asked *Kansas City (KS) Sun* editor A.W. Stubbs. After Stubbs received a long rebuttal to the "insidious and dastardly propaganda" explaining that Catholics occupied only 5 percent of public offices, the editor concluded, "If the K.K.K. organization is based on false premises, as the figures given indicate, then all this tirade against the Catholic church and the Knights of Columbus is pure bunc and the loyal people of this country will soon see that such an organization has no legitimate place among American institutions." But Stubbs fell for the Klan's "bunc" in September 1924. By this time, the order had been in Kansas City for almost four years. Stubb's naiveté illustrates the effectiveness of Klan propaganda on local opinion leaders.[150]

Klansman E.L. Brown, pastor of the Central Methodist Church, was an exception of sorts to the Klan's vigorous anti-Catholicism. Brown left Kansas City for a Garnett, Kansas church in 1923. Still publicly identifying himself as a "proud" Klansman, he nevertheless forged a relationship with local Catholics. Klan and Catholic met jointly at the Anderson County Courthouse in September 1923 to discuss city conditions. "One man in the audience said the world is coming to an end. The lion and the lamb have laid down together. But who is the lamb?" asked the *Garnett (KS) Republican-Plaindealer*, demonstrating the same ambivalence as Governor Allen to the two organizations.[151]

Garnett had been lately disturbed by "radicals who have been invading the neighborhood and stirring up the usually peaceful community to strife and hatred," reported the *Fort Scott (KS) Tribune*. The Catholics and Klansmen "talked things over in a conciliatory way" and passed resolutions condemning the trouble. But the article was vague. The radicals went unnamed, as did their specific actions, although leftist union organizers may have been the cause of concern. The meeting "was based upon the broad ground of religious liberty. The resolutions call attention to the unrest and misery in Europe and emphasize the desire to avoid such a condition in the United States," the *Tribune* noted.[152]

Catholics did not exactly turn the other cheek during the Klan's anti-Catholic revival. Church leaders, however, carefully responded to the aspersions and attacks on their faith. Knights of Columbus state deputy James Malone worried that too forceful a Catholic reaction would make the bigotry worse. Malone decided the best strategy was to avoid direct conflict with the Klan. Instead, Catholics should defend their faith with the truth. The Knights of Columbus thus concentrated on fighting the Klan's circulation of the bogus oath. They placed advertisements in papers across the state offering a $25,000 reward to anyone who could prove the oath's authenticity. No one was awarded the cash, but the campaign helped the Knights educate their fellow citizens on the true contents of the organization's oath. The authentic oath always appeared in full along with the reward notice.[153]

The Knights of Columbus battled other anti-Catholic myths. A popular fable of the time disclosed how Catholic fathers donated a rifle to the church arsenal every time they had a new baby boy. The weapons were at the ready, awaiting only the Pope's order for a general Catholic uprising. Credulous elderly Protestants confessed to the author they once took the arms tale as gospel.

Kansas City Klansmen inherited their country's historic suspicion of Catholic loyalties and combined it with a new understanding of race to make their "Papist" neighbors utterly unassimilable. Interpreted in the context of Klan plans for the city, Roman Catholics were seen as yet another obstacle in their fight to unify Kansas City under their banner.

Thousands of Kansas City's white, native-born Protestants joined the KKK in 1921 with the hope of addressing the city's longstanding problems of civic unity, progress and regional autonomy on their terms. When the Knights of the Ku Klux Klan lost its ability to aid in that effort, members left in droves, including 450 in a single day. But the search for an acceptable way to utilize "100 Percent Americanism, Protestant Christianity, and White

Supremacy" in their campaign to capture the city was only beginning. Former Klansmen attempted three revisions of the order, never differing over ends but rather "methods and operations." Erasing the "objectionable features" of the boycott and class hatred, as well as secrecy, residual "southerness" and autocratic organization, Kansas City Klansmen designed what they believed were "unobjectionable" orders. But their opponents saw things differently. With the exception of the Knights of America, no Klan organization from Colorado, Georgia, Kansas or Indiana was ever chartered to operate legally in the state. Notwithstanding the fears of masked political competition, the ongoing ouster suit (which would run from July 18, 1922, to February 28, 1927) gave state officials a ready excuse to reject the applications of any Klan or Klan-related organization.

The one reform the Klan could not endure was the only reform that would have made it acceptable to elected officials: its absolute dissolution. But the Klan's refusal to reform itself ideologically would also contribute to its eventual decline in Kansas City. With a Catholic population of nearly thirty thousand, any hope of true unity, progress and autonomy was doomed without their participation. Antipathy to Rome was so ingrained in the Klan mentality, however, that its elimination was never considered a reform.

5
KITH KIN KLAN

PART I. WHO?

Who were the Kansas Citians hidden inside the robes and masks of the Klan and its imitators? Who were those normal people doing abnormal things—libeling Roman Catholics, terrorizing African Americans and abusing their official positions to advance Wyandotte Klan No. 5's agenda? A representative "normal" member of Klan No. 5 is Thomas Younger Baird, and his profession certainly made joining the Klan an abnormal thing to do.

Tom Baird was the longest-serving team owner and executive in Negro League baseball history. It was some team. The Kansas City Monarchs were the New York Yankees of black baseball—although, it is more accurate to state that the Yankees were the Monarchs of the all-white major leagues. Legendary players Satchel Paige, Bullet Joe Rogan, Buck O'Neil, Jackie Robinson and more starred for the Monarchs during the Baird years.

He was born in 1885 in Madison County, Arkansas. The family moved to Kansas City when Baird was a teen and settled in the Armourdale district. A good semipro ballplayer, Baird had to give up playing the game after damaging his leg in a railroad accident. A limp marked his walk thereafter. He left the tracks to open a pool hall and bowling alley. He remained active in baseball as a manager and promoter. He started the Monarchs in 1919 with J.L. Wilkinson, beginning a partnership that lasted nearly thirty years.[154]

Klansman Tom Baird (*left*) and fellow baseball men C.A. Franklin (*center*) and J.L. Wilkinson (*right*) discuss the future of Negro League baseball. *Spencer Research Library.*

Baird and Wilkinson ran the Monarchs according to their abilities. The empathetic "Wilkie," as general manager, spent his time with the players, building remarkably close personal bonds. It was said he was the most popular white man in black America. Tall, lean Tom Baird, whose austere mien did not suggest easy intimacy, covered the business end of the operation, booking games and making deals. Baird spent so much time behind the scenes that some early Monarchs players never knew he owned part of the club.[155]

Baird bought Wilkinson's interest in the team in 1948 to become the Monarchs' sole owner. He held onto the team as long as he could, but Negro League baseball faded with the reintegration of the major leagues with Jackie Robinson. Baird sold the Monarchs in 1955 but continued in the sports business with semipro baseball teams, basketball teams, as well as his pool halls and bowling alleys.[156]

Baird's private papers, on deposit in a university library, are full of evidence documenting personal, social, business and political ties with fellow kluxers. He not only broke bread with other Klan members, he also breathed the same air. His home on Grandview Boulevard, purchased from Klansman Homer D. McCallum in 1921, sat on the same block as the homes of Klansmen George Scherer, Dr. Cresse P. Rhoads and Albert L. McCallum. The Boyns Hall building in the 1700 block of Central Avenue, where Baird ran a pool hall and kept a business office, also housed the local headquarters of Wyandotte Klan No. 5 and the women's Kamelia Kourt Klan order. Dr. Rhoads, a dentist, had his practice there, as did the Baird family physician, Dr. J.W. Sparks, whose name also appears on the Klan list. Another Klan member in the building was William W. Maze, a longtime Baird associate and employee who managed one of his bowling enterprises.[157]

Later in his career, Baird's Klan world spread east past the state line into the heart of Kansas City, Missouri's historic African American district with his purchase of 1832 and 1824 Vine Street. He insured his new holdings through agent Harold O. Tinklepaugh, whose name is also on the Klan roster. A parking lot now occupies the property. It sits diagonally from the Negro Leagues Baseball Museum. Tom Baird owned not only the Kansas City Monarchs but also part of its neighborhood, the world-famous Eighteenth and Vine.[158]

Outside of business, he was a lodge man—the Order of Red Men, in his case—and a "mainline" Christian who attended a Disciples of Christ church. Baird took an interest in civic and political affairs. He was a director of the Grandview Improvement Association. Baird joined thirteen fellow Klan-tied candidates to make up nearly a third of the field running for the new Kansas City Board of Public Utilities in 1929. His candidacy failed, but he did find some measure of political power when he was appointed to the Kansas City City Planning Board in 1954. Tom Baird died in 1962. He was not an obscure figure in Negro Leagues baseball history, but he did not win the acclaim of his former business partner Wilkinson, who was inducted into the National Baseball Hall of Fame in 2006.[159]

Baird is one of nearly a thousand Kansas City men revealed in a Ku Klux Klan membership roster discovered at the Library of Congress in the papers of former Kansas governor Henry J. Allen, an ardent foe of the hooded order. Dated November 13, 1922, the Klan list confirms the normal, "average" middle-class impression left by Baird and other members of the Invisible Empire on their earliest observers.[160]

By the numbers, most members were slightly less than middle-aged at 35.3 years old, married (N=614 or 68.7 percent) and owned their homes (N=515 or 57.6 percent). Place of residence augmented ties of class and workplace. Almost half of the men (N=440 or 49.2 percent) lived on the same block as

Eight Klansmen lived on the 900 block of Kansas Avenue in the Armourdale neighborhood. Most of the homes are gone now. *Author's collection.*

another Klansman. Some Kansas City streets had as many as six Klansmen on a single block. More frequently, three, four and five Klansmen lived on the same block. Kansas City's thickest "Klan block" was located on the 900 block of Armourdale's Kansas Avenue, which hosted eight Klan members, including some of its most active leaders.[161]

No Klansmen lived in the city's First Ward, a northeast Kansas City section that has traditionally hosted nonwhite residents. The Second Ward had 16 Klansmen. The Third Ward embraced the largest number of Klan, non-Klan and African American citizens; 302 Klansmen dwelled in the Third. The Fourth and Fifth Wards were the city's central wards in the 1920s; 269 Klansmen lived there. In Armourdale, the Sixth Ward, were 71 Klansmen. There were 120 Klansmen in the Seventh Ward, Argentine, where the Klan became so popular that by 1925 the neighborhood had its own chapter. No residence was determined for 116 members. Rosedale became the city's Eighth Ward in 1922. Rosedale Klan No. 17's 200 Klansmen were led by Lawrence E. Wilson and David F. Espenlaub, the latter a county commissioner. No. 17 remained a separate klavern throughout the Klan era.[162]

Klansmen lived in the same wards, neighborhoods and occasionally in the same house or apartment as another member. A total of 95 men shared an address with another Klansman. Of these, 47 had the same surname; 10 were coworkers. Kinship enhanced the organization's cohesion. In addition, 88 Klansmen strengthened family ties with Klan membership; numerous father-son, brother-brother and father-in-law–and–son-in-law combinations were identified. Furthermore, 232 Klansmen shared a surname with at least 1 other member.[163]

Most Klansmen residing in Kansas City were born in Kansas or Missouri. Other fertile states for producing Klan members were Illinois, Iowa, Ohio, Nebraska and Indiana. Combined with members from Kansas and Missouri, men from these states composed 86 percent of the Kansas City membership. The Klan may have had southern roots, but most of its Kansas City chapter did not. Tom Baird was an exception.[164]

Despite the Klan's "native-born" membership requirement, three Kansas City members were foreign born, with one member each from Germany, Northern Ireland and Scotland. The Scot had immigrated to the United States in 1915. Records show that 248 Klan parents were also foreign born, with Germany providing 35 percent of that number and the United Kingdom about 25 percent.[165]

Klansmen served in their country's conflicts. More than 150 members performed service in the Great War; this is more than 16 percent of the identified membership. Police night captain Stanley Beatty fought with the Tank Corps in France. He became Kansas City's youngest detective when he returned from the war. At thirty-two, Beatty was also the youngest police captain in the United States. An elderly Klansman experienced battle with the Union army in the Civil War. This is almost as puzzling as the membership of William G. Bird, whose father was killed by Missouri (pro-Confederate) bushwhackers in 1865. Police day captain Ulysses Grant Snyder claimed to have been an "Indian fighter" during his western Kansas boyhood. A total of 15 members fought in the Spanish-American War, 1 in the Philippines insurrection and 1 saw Mexican Border Service against Pancho Villa. In addition, 7 Klansmen served in the peacetime army or navy. A Klansman died on active duty in 1940 when the United States began a readiness draft before entering World War II. And 1 Klansman claimed a religious exemption from service when he registered for the draft in World War I. Klan veterans led both the local American Legion and the United Spanish War Veterans chapters in the 1920s.[166]

Most Kansas City Klansmen (51.7 percent) worked with at least one fellow member. Twenty-five Klan businessmen employed fellow Knights. Kansas City's top ten employers of Klansmen included: Armour and Company, thirty-two; the City of Kansas City, forty-eight; Chicago, Rock Island and Pacific Railroad, twenty-six; Kansas City Railway Company, twenty-four; Kansas City Structural Steel, fifteen; Atchison, Topeka and Santa Fe Railroad, ninety-five; Swift and Company, seventeen; the U.S. government, seventeen; Union Pacific Railroad, eleven; and Wyandotte County, eleven. The top ten employers of Kansas City Klansmen comprised one-third of the order's members.[167]

Life in the Invisible Empire introduced its members to like-minded businessmen. Anecdotal newspaper notices document the buying and selling of grocery stores, drugstores, shoe stores and confectioneries among fellow Klansmen. Medical practice partnerships combining Klan doctors were also reported. The partnerships formed after the Klan organized in the city.

The Klan dominated some Kansas City quarters. The city's South District Court was thoroughly kluxed. Judge Don C. McCombs, Chief Deputy Clerk James P. Fox, Junior Clerk Bina S. Quick Jr., Marshal Charles E. Pointer and Deputy Marshal Charles Langford were members.[168]

Klansmen filled other local organizations. "No thinking person has ever seriously considered the suggestion that Masonry was fostering Ku Kluxism," the *Catholic Register* ventured, "but it has long been evident that a certain assertive element in Masonry was excellent material for membership in the Klan." Kansas City had one of the highest per capita percentages of Masonic order membership in the country, claiming more than 10,000 members. If accurate, that means members of the various Masonic orders made up nearly 10 percent of the city's population. Visiting a city's lodges was a kleagle's first priority when attempting to "klux" a community. The high number of Masons who joined the Klan reflects this recruiting strategy perhaps as much as the organization's historic anti-Catholicism. Either way, Kansas City's fraternal lodges offered the Klan thousands of prospects and hundreds of members.[169]

Wyandotte Klan No. 5 members were scattered throughout Kansas City's lodge community. Photographs of Klansmen who led fraternal groups crowded papers from the era, including that of Dr. H.O. Mailer. He organized a "Grotto" of two hundred Masons, 30 percent of whom were also members of the Klan. Wyandotte Lodge No. 3, the oldest Masonic lodge in the state, also shared members with the Klan. But more important, No. 3 gave the Klan experienced leadership, as three of its former leaders—DeVirda H. Burcham, Richard R. Fleck and Walter H Williams—became the first three exalted cyclops of Wyandotte Klan No. 5.[170]

Burcham, Fleck and Williams were united in denominational allegiance as well. Their families attended the First Baptist Church at Tenth and Grandview Streets. Church records are not available for every Klan member, but the records that survive all point to the Protestant mainline. Kansas City Klansmen were Northern Baptists, Congregationalists, Disciples of Christ, Episcopalians, Lutherans, Methodists and Presbyterians. Fundamentalist churches were a minority in Kansas City during the Klan era. The Assembly of God, the Church of the Nazarene and the Church of Christ, for example, mustered a total of only 359 members and five congregations in Kansas City in the 1920s.[171]

Numerous Kansas City clergymen joined or supported the Klan. The Reverends E.L. Brown and A.J. Morton pastored Methodist churches. The Reverend George W. Durham, a Methodist, and N.V. Tatum, a Congregationalist, whose names do not appear on the extant Klan rosters, were nevertheless so pro-Klan that official membership would have been redundant. Reverend David T. Cruden, a Disciples of Christ minister, was a member and ardent supporter of the order from the pulpit. Dr. W.E. Brandenberg, another Disciples minister, conducted Sunday afternoon worship services at the Klan lodge. Reverend Charles H. Reed of the Westheights Methodist Episcopal Church also spoke at Klan meetings.[172]

The only known Klan funeral held in the Kansas City area was conducted by Reverend Harry Smith, First Christian Church, and Reverend W.D. Bigour, First Methodist Episcopal Church, of nearby Bonners Springs. They officiated at the service of Frank Alden, a well-known funeral home director. The September 1924 ceremony featured 140 Klansmen from klaverns in Bonner Springs and Shawnee, Kansas, in full regalia. The men formed an honor guard around Alden's hearse and then encircled his grave during interment. The Klansmen sang a hymn, after which a fellow member gave a short sermon. More than 700 mourners attended Alden's funeral service. Among them was the deceased's brother Dell, exalted cyclops of Shawnee Klan No. 32.[173]

Pro-Klan churches, those defined as either making positive public statements about the order or welcoming robed and masked Klan visitors to their services, included the First Christian Church, Central Methodist Episcopal, London Heights Methodist Episcopal, Quindaro Christian,

Leavenworth Klansmen gather at church for a Klan funeral. Wyandotte County held its first Klan burial service in 1924. *Kansas Historical Society.*

Trinity English Lutheran, State Avenue Baptist, Immanuel Baptist, Chelsea Baptist, Chelsea Christian, Advent Christian (which would one day host the Junior Klan), University United Brethren and the Welborn Community (Congregational) church. These churches were socially directed and committed to establishing the Kingdom of God on earth through good works.[174]

Klan clergymen preached the "Social Gospel" of earthly political and other reforms more than the "old time religion" of the fundamentalists. The *Kansas City (KS) Labor Bulletin* beamed of one Klan parson: "Reverend [E.L.] Brown can always be depended on to be upon the side of fairness and the working people. His religion is the kind that has to do with problems we have to meet here in this world. He preaches a gospel of better wages, better conditions and better homes while we are here in this world. Some pastors of the wealthy churches would have the poor people wait until they got to heaven to get what is due them."[175]

The Reverend George W. Durham also received praise from the labor organ: "Rev. Durham analyzed the fault of the Industrial Court [a special court to adjudicate labor disputes in place of strikes] in a very logical way by pointing out that the proper solution as he thought, is to strike at the heart of the whole matter, which is coal itself, and the way to do that is for the coal operator and the coal miner to be the same person through the state owning the mines." Durham was really saying the "heart of the whole matter" was capitalism itself. This was further than most Kansas City workers were willing to go in 1921 and certainly was not a goal of the Klan. It illustrates, however, the degree to which historians of the Klan have erred in depicting the order as kneejerk defenders of free-market capitalism.[176]

Reverend N.M. Tatum put a career of community leadership to the service of the Klan. Tatum fostered the organization of two Klan auxiliaries, the Knights of America in 1922 and the Kansas Law Enforcement League in 1925. The league was formed following the death of twelve-year-old Thelma Sloan by a drunk driver. Assisted by Klan members, Tatum and the Reverend Durham spoke at churches throughout the city recruiting members for the league. One hundred members joined at Immanuel Baptist Church in June; three hundred more joined the following week at the State Avenue Baptist Church. Two Klansmen who escorted Tatum became Christians during the service. In October 1927, Tatum brought Reverend Charles Sheldon to Kansas City. The progressive Topeka Congregationalist famously asked, "What would Jesus do?" in his bestselling book *In His Steps*. Sheldon's lecture on the possibility of world peace drew seven hundred attendees. Sheldon was hardly the fare of fundamentalist or even conservative Christians, but he did appeal to mainline Protestants, including supporters of the Ku Klux Klan.[177]

A Christian, a family man, a homeowner, a lodge member. A small-business owner, a skilled craftsman, a clerk. A neighbor, a cousin, a brother, a coworker, a boss, an employee, a business partner. A partisan, a booster, a lover of his city—or at least what he thought his city should be. Of these normal ties of kith and kin a Klansman was made.

Part II. How Many?

Tom Baird and his fellow Klansmen on Governor Allen's list represent an unknown quantum of total area Klan strength. True Klan membership numbers are difficult to find. Both the Klan and its enemies had reasons to inflate the count. The specter of a large Klan benefited both parties. In February 1922, local papers reported rumors that Wyandotte Klan No. 5 had five thousand members in the city. In late April 1922, in a letter to Reverend George W. Durham, the organization claimed seven thousand

"One-Hundred Percent Americans" in its ranks. But Klan strength at the time of the order's boast to Durham in the spring of 1922 was probably much lower than seven thousand.[178]

On July 13, 1922, 450 men left the Klan in protest of Exalted Cyclops DeVirda H. Burcham's alleged plans to punish school superintendent Matthew E. Pearson. The following spring, Burcham's successor as chapter president, Walter H. Williams, testified in a state lawsuit against the Klan that the "last report showed about 650 members paid up." This amounts to approximately 1,100 Klansmen. The membership roster obtained by the office of Governor Henry J. Allen in November lists 1,053 names, including those who had quit in July. The number 1,100 was pretty accurate in 1922, at least in Kansas City proper.[179]

Additional Klan chapters in the city and county also contributed members to the local Klan sheet count, although specifics are rare. No. 5 had organizational jurisdiction over all seven of Kansas City's wards until the addition of Rosedale as the city's Eighth Ward in June 1922, which had already formed Rosedale Klan No. 17 and remained independent. Klan strength in the city's Seventh Ward of Argentine would grow so great that Argentine Klan No. 90 would appear as a separate chapter in 1925. Nearby Bonner Springs Klan No. 9 formed in 1922. A membership roster for No. 9 names about one hundred men.[180]

Local papers reported the occasional Klan initiation ceremony and the number of new citizens "naturalized" into the Invisible Empire. Two hundred men from Wyandotte and adjacent Johnson Counties joined in a De Soto, Kansas ceremony in August 1924. Another one hundred took the oath in De Soto that fall as eight thousand Klansmen and other observers from the region paid witness. Three public ceremonies in 1927 added an additional five hundred members to Klan No. 5.[181]

Klan parades hint at the order's strength in the city. In November 1926, 1,500 kluxers marched up Minnesota Avenue. A year later, 2,500 robed Klansman from the area took to the streets with an additional 2,500 members in mufti filling the sidewalks. To complicate the headcount, Kansas City Klan parades included members from outside Wyandotte County and the state of Kansas.[182]

Other public Klan events offer clues of the Invisible Empire's popularity in Kansas City. The order commenced a series of sixteen weekly lectures in the summer of 1925; 1,400 attended the inaugural speech by state Klan lecturer W.F. Woodward. A mixed Klan chorus of 50 Klansmen and 50 Klanswomen provided musical entertainment. Two thousand attended the next week's talk "given…to law enforcement and the duty of the citizens to take a more active interest in voting and in law enforcement," the *Kansan* reported. The crowd at the Emma Thayer-Magee Tabernacle required Klan-robed traffic directors on the street to ease the congestion. Electric crosses buzzed above the building's interior and exterior walls. Membership cards were collected at the end of each program. Prospective members who completed the "katechesis" were sworn into the Klan at the next lecture.[183]

Local papers teemed with news of Klan events throughout 1925. In late August, the *Kansan* reported that eight thousand people attended a public meeting at the Lee Brown farm, twelve miles west of Kansas City, to hear Reverend E.E. Edwards of Leavenworth dilate on patriotism. The paper announced plans for a joint meeting of all four Wyandotte county Klans—Kansas City, Rosedale, Argentine and Bonner Springs—in September, which promised to attract fifteen thousand members, although no further news ever verified the crowd claim. In 1928, Klan members met at the Welborn Community Church to discuss the fall's election. The event drew two thousand Klan citizens.[184]

Minstrel shows featuring white folks in blackface were a common form of entertainment in 1920s Kansas City. Business, church, fraternal and school groups routinely offered the fare for their own amusement or as fundraisers. Ku Klux Klan minstrel shows at Memorial Hall drew crowds of sixteen hundred persons.[185]

The Klan's annual summer picnics also illustrate the order's strength in Wyandotte County. A reported thirty-two thousand picnic-goers attended the Klan's Fourth of July party in Bonner Springs in 1925. Wyandotte Klan No. 5 did not sponsor the picnic until 1928, when the chapter's thirty-two-piece band and drill team performed. A Klan beauty contest was also among the festivities. An estimated twenty-five thousand Klansmen and their families from a 150-mile radius attended the 1928 party. There is reason to doubt these numbers, however, as the estimates by the local press varied greatly from "several thousand" to the twenty-five thousand to thirty-two thousand noted here. The annual picnics included Klans from Kansas City, Leavenworth, Tonganoxie, Linwood and De Soto, Kansas, among others. The events were open to the public and heavily publicized. Once again, the admixture of Klanfolk and non-Klan visitors from across the region makes it difficult to count the Wyandotte County numbers accurately. Nostalgia for the "old stock" communities of the past helps explain the popularity of the picnics with Klan and non-Klan members

Plainclothes Klansmen erecting a cross before an evening's revelries. *Library of Congress.*

alike. Social events always attracted more Klanfolk than the order's ritual exercises or more nefarious activities.[186]

If the heavy attendance at Klan public events does not translate to actual Klan membership numbers, it does illustrate the Klan's appeal and its ability to attract other citizens into a larger, if unorganized, Klan movement. Klansman Harry Lillich's independent candidacy for sheriff in 1922 was supported in a petition by "8,000 working men and their wives" and by 9,000 voters in the election. Although Lillich reportedly resigned his Klan membership to pursue the office, he was the acknowledged Klan candidate. Similarly, DeVirda H. Burcham, George W. Durham and Bert R. Collins received close vote totals in both primary and general elections of nearly 10,000 votes apiece. Non-Klan citizens also supported Klan-led initiatives to remove the Argentine High School dancing instructor for promoting "jazz" dancing and in opposing integrated school events. Non-Klan support of the Klan is similar to the support one might give a politician because of a single issue even while rejecting the candidate's party or platform.[187]

WOMEN OF THE KU KLUX KLAN
ARE NOW ENLISTING
100% AMERICAN WOMEN

——————

For Information Write
V. R. C. Box 573, Pittsburgh, Pa.

Even Klanswomen need calling cards. *Author's collection.*

Klansmen dominated coverage of the Klan in Kansas City, but women joined the order's ladies' auxiliary. The women's order remained active throughout the 1920s. The market for a women's Klan was evident in 1922 when a satirical account of a "Ku Klux Klannette" church visit appeared in the *Kansan*. "The women presented the Reverend F.W. May of the University United Brethren church with a purse, $1, Saturday night. It was at the height of a party which the Rev. and Mrs. May were giving at their home…for the Christian Endeavor Society that a group of weird hooded figures silently stalked into the room. A hush fell on the merrymakers. One of the shrouded figures stepped forward and in a hushed voice made the presentation speech. Then as silently as the number had come, so they moved away….Unmasked, the band proved to be the Women's Bible Class and the Criterion Class."[188]

University United Brethren Church was among the churches that welcomed the Klan when it made its church visits in early 1922. The Klannettes obviously robed in jest, but Kansas City women were soon wearing the sheet as full-fledged members of a Klan order.

Kamelia Kourt No. 27 initiated four hundred Kansas City women into its mysteries in July 1923 in a pasture near the intersection of Fortieth Street and Wood Avenue, the *Kansan* reported. Several thousand additional women witnessed the ceremony, which was conducted by two Klansmen under the light of a burning cross.[189]

The Kamelia were another creation of Klan founder William Joseph Simmons, who exploited the Klan's dawdling on the organization of a ladies' auxiliary to start his own. The rivalry between the Kamelia and

KU KLUX KREED

WE, the Order of the Women of the Ku Klux Klan, reverentially acknowledge the majesty and supremacy of Almighty God a n d recognize His goodness and providence through Jesus Christ our Lord.

Recognizing our relation to the government of the United States of America, the Supremacy of its Constitution, the Union of States thereunder, and the Constitutional Laws thereof, we shall ever be devoted to the sublime principles of a pure Americanism, and valiant in the defense of its ideals and institutions.

We avow the distinction between the races of mankind as decreed by the Creator, and we shall ever he true to the maintenance of White Supremacy and strenuously oppose any compromise thereof.

We appreciate the value of practical, fraternal relationship among people of kindred thought, purpose and ideals and the infinite benefits accruing therefrom, we shall faithfully devote ourselves to the practice of an honorable clannishness that the life of each may be a constant blessing to others.

"Non Silba Sed Anthar"

The Kreed of the Women's Ku Klux Klan was identical to the men's creed. *Author's collection.*

97

the emerging Women's Ku Klux Klan forced another legal battle between Simmons and his rivals. Once again Simmons left the white sheet scene with a bountiful payout. Often ridiculed for alleged incompetence by the press, by his rivals and now by scholars, Simmons found profit at every twist and turn of the Klan's serpentine history.[190]

Kamelia national president Grace J. Jones said the order, which had formed only in March 1923, was already organized in seventeen states and had enrolled 500,000 members into its secret ranks. Despite paterfamilias Simmons's creation of the Kamelia, Jones was quick to add, "The Kamelias will work in spirit with the principle of the Klan but will not conduct their work jointly with the male organization."[191]

Their independence from the men's order may explain their relative absence from the news; Klansmen were the story in the male-dominated society of the early twentieth century. The 1923 initiation article is part of the scant evidence documenting the presence of female kluxers in Kansas City.

The Kamelias are out of the papers until 1925, when Miss Thelma Higgins, daughter of Klansman Claude Higgins, spoke on the order's behalf at the summer's annual Klan picnic. Kamelias appeared in the paper again when one hundred members visited Reverend Tatum's Welborn Community Church with a donation of fifty dollars to aid the church's revival. The

Form J-401

HONOR IS THE CROWNING VIRTURE OF AMERICAN MANHOOD

Your friends state you are a native-born American, having the best interest of your community, city, state and nation at heart, owing no allegiance to any foreign government, sect, creed or ruler, and believe in:

The Tenets of the Christian Religion.
White Supremacy.
Protection of our pure womanhood.
Just laws and liberty.
Closer relationship of pure American-ism.
The upholding of the Constitution of these United States.
The separation of Church and State.
Freedom of speech, press and peaceful assembly.

Closer relationship between capital and American labor.
Preventing the causes of mob violence and lynchings.
Preventing unwarranted strikes by foreign agitators.
Prevention of fires and destruction of property by lawless elements.
The limitation of foreign immigration.
Much needed local reforms.
The strict enforcement of all laws.

BOYS whose honor and character are above reproach are needed.
Upon these beliefs and the recommendations of your friends you are given an opportunity to become a member of the most powerful secret organization in existence for the youth of America. "FOR GOD AND COUNTRY, FATHER AND MOTHER."

100 Percent American boys joined the Junior KKK, headquartered in Kansas City, Missouri. *Author's collection.*

women were adorned in white robes. The Kamelias' final newspaper notice came in July 1928, when they met at the home of Mrs. Homer Applegarth to honor the visiting national president of the Kamelia Kourt.[192]

A Junior Ku Klux Klan formed in Kansas City, Missouri, in October 1924. The order's national headquarters resided in the city. The youngsters' Klan was open to boys of "good character" and the right pedigree. The Junior Klan promised "beautiful ritualistic work, [a] splendid environment, teaching [of] the great principles of Klancraft, and preparing the boys for a better citizenship."[193]

A June 1925 initiation ceremony at the "Klan park" in Tonganoxie brought three hundred boys together for a picnic, field day and "naturalization ceremony." The *Kansan* reported the boys came from Kansas City, Missouri, and Tonganoxie, Kansas City, Topeka, Lawrence, Leavenworth, Linwood, De Soto and Bonner Springs, Kansas. A few months later, the Junior Klan appeared in public for the first time in Kansas City when they entered the Advent Christian Church at Twenty-Fourth Street and Garfield Avenue to present an American flag to the pastor. The boys then led the congregation in the Pledge of Allegiance. The paper did not divulge their names, so we know even less about them than the two Klanswomen named by the *Kansan*.[194]

The exact number of women, boys and "average" men who joined the sundry orders of the KKK in Kansas City cannot be counted with confidence. A total of three thousand is reasonable, with another ten thousand nonmembers who supported known Klan political candidates, and perhaps another ten thousand to fifteen thousand citizens who never said no to a free picnic lunch, lecture or minstrel show.

6

POLITICS

ike a Trojan horse in a white sheet, the Ku Klux Klan consolidated congenial office seekers and officeholders under its cover and entered city gates. Although Republicans were in the saddle, the hooded order backed any candidate who backed it. The Klan and its candidates would be at the center of city and county politics for most of the decade, and beyond.

Some of the men who joined the Klan already knew the halls of power. Republican William Beggs served as county assessor in 1910 and county clerk from 1918 to 1930. Beggs was among the men observed at the May 4, 1922 Klan meeting reported by the *Catholic Register*. Klansman William G. Bird's Republican career stretched from 1882 to 1930 as precinct committeeman, county assessor and county treasurer. Other veteran politicians who appear in the Klan records include Republicans U. Grant Gates, Justus N. Baird, E.A. Enright, Richard R. Fleck, Thomas C. Hattley, J.W. Hayward, Don C. McCombs, William L. Wood and W.J. Wright Jr.[195]

William G. Bird's political calling came early. At age sixteen, he organized Kansas City's bootblacks and newsboys for T.B. Bullene in the 1882 race for mayor of Kansas City, Missouri. By age thirty-two, he was the state labor commissioner of Kansas, where he lobbied for the elimination of his own office.[196]

Veteran Democrats T.A. Powell and Louis S. Harvey joined their partisan opponents in the Klan. Harvey came from a prominent political family. His brother Colonel A.M. Harvey was the Populist lieutenant governor of

Kansas in the 1890s. Another brother, W.W. Harvey, was a former speaker of the Kansas House of Representatives and state supreme court judge.[197]

The Klan inspired new candidates, too. Eighty-two Klansmen entered politics after they joined the Invisible Empire. The new men were mostly Republicans, but twelve Democrats and six nonpartisan candidates also emerged from Klan ranks. The Klan-born candidates ran for forty-six offices between 1921 and 1930, winning thirteen. Reverend George W. Durham and D.M. Boddington gained seats on the board of education. David F. Espenlaub and Frank Werner became county commissioners. Fledgling Klan candidates also won eighty-five precinct committeemen slots during those years.[198]

The one positive Klan political result discovered during the writing of this book was the 1925 leadership of Commissioner Espenlaub as he worked with the Argentine Activities Association to add railway service across the Twelfth Street Bridge. Representing the activities association were Dr. K.C. Haas and Lester Gilmore, both members of Wyandotte Klan No. 5. The next year, Gilmore won a seat in the state legislature.[199]

Altogether, over the Klan decade of the 1920s, No. 5 candidates old and new ran in 125 popular campaigns, winning 56 races and losing 79. This number includes primary and general election contests. In the more meaningful results of general elections only, Kansas City Klansmen won 28 times. Combined with their 102 precinct committee captaincies, Kansas City Klansmen captured 130 democratically elected offices.[200]

Politics was local to the Klan. Its candidates sought city and county offices over larger spheres of state. The white, native-born Protestant revival began at home. Klan political plans began well. No. 5's mayoral candidate William W. Gordon in 1923 easily defeated Mayor Burton, the Klan's biggest foe. The hooded order had the momentum to take over the city. But its progress, as well as the progress of the greater Klan across the state, continued to be checked by the state ouster suit began by former governor Henry Allen. The suit forced Klan chapters to fight on two fronts: one in their local community, and one the width and breadth of Kansas.[201]

The ouster suit produced a "finding of fact" in late April 1924 that the KKK must have a state charter to operate legally in Kansas. The charter could only be obtained by a two-thirds vote of the state charter board. The board was composed of Attorney General Charles B. Griffith, Secretary of State Frank J. Ryan and State Bank Commissioner Roy L. Bone. Griffith and Ryan were faced with reelection that year. Both men were stridently anti-Klan.[202]

Republican Ben S. Paulen and Democrat governor Jonathon M. Davis were the only major gubernatorial contestants. Both men were also rumored to be friendly to the Klan. Paulen had even received the Klan's endorsement for the office. (Former mayor Burton challenged Davis in the Democratic primary because of the issue and lost.) Anti-Klan Kansans feared that if Paulen and Davis ignored the Klan question in the general election, pro-Klan voters would have sufficient electoral strength to capture the charter board and thereby solve its legal problems.[203]

The most vocal exponent of this scenario was the famous Emporia newspaper editor William Allen White. On September 20, 1924, the prominent Republican declared for the governor's race as an independent candidate, announcing, "I want to offer Kansans afraid of the Klan and ashamed of that disgrace, a candidate who shares their fear and shame." But White's run for the statehouse was brusquely dismissed by most Kansas City Republicans. He was tainted by his association with the *Kansas City Star*. Far from the principled anti-Klan image that White and his supporters would later cultivate, contemporary skeptics interpreted the Emporian's entry into the race as a mere attempt to inject a "progressive" Republican candidate into the fray and steal the office from the party's regular "stand pat" faction. In the event, Paulen won the office. White received nearly 150,000 votes. The incumbent Davis finished only 30,000 votes ahead of White.[204]

William Allen White, however, did not win all the votes he expected. Kansas City's Republican "blackbelt" of African American voters remained loyal to the GOP in 1924. "Lacking any genuine ground for his attack on Paulen, he [White] raises the fake Klan issue, while privately admitting that he cares nothing about the Klan one way or the other," charged the *Kansas City (KS) Advocate*, an African American Republican weekly. Furthermore, African Americans, Republicans or Democrats, saw nothing substantial to gain in supporting a third-party candidate. In the harsh political world of the 1920s, they were lucky to hold on to the meager thirty-odd jobs awarded by patronage. White could not win, so White could not deliver. White also failed to win most Roman Catholics to his anti-Klan crusade. Like his friend Henry Allen, the former anti-Klan, anti-Catholic Kansas governor, White viewed the Catholic Church with the same side-eye suspicion he laid on the Klan.[205]

Unlike White, Governor Davis did win thousands of African American and Catholic votes in his failed reelection run. Reverend A.S. Mayfield's Church of the Living God passed a resolution in support of Davis "because of the Klan issue," taking him for his word that he was against the hooded order.[206]

The famous Emporia, Kansas journalist William Allen White ran for governor in 1924 as a protest against Republican and Democratic candidates he thought insufficiently anti-Klan. *Library of Congress.*

Despite White's personal flaws and his defeat in the 1924 election, his campaign was not a failure. "I got out and challenged it and rebuked it and stopped it from proving its power by defeating Ryan, Griffith, and Miley [the state superintendent of education]," White said. "That protest and the triumph of the three men on the Republican ticket, whom the Klan was fighting, broke the back of the Klan." Whatever his true intentions and impact in the 1924 election, White was right—the Klan was damaged.[207]

Pro-Klan Kansas legislators introduced Senate Bill 269 in January 1925 to grant the hooded order the elusive charter required to operate legally in the state. *Kansas Historical Society*.

The Kansas supreme court confirmed the ouster suit's "finding of fact" on January 10, 1925, and ruled that the "Ku Klux Klan is ousted from organizing or controlling lodges…in the state." The Klan was on the ropes in Kansas, but despite the victories of Griffith and Ryan, the order still had a promising course of redress. The new (1925) legislature included numerous pro-Klan members. On February 25, 1925, it passed S. 269, the "Klan bill," through the state senate, twenty-three to fourteen. The bill would have recognized the Klan by automatically granting it the elusive charter. Anti-Klan forces led by House Speaker Clifford R. Hope, however, outmaneuvered the Klan's legislative supporters and narrowly defeated the bill in the lower chamber.[208]

Hope's defeat of the Klan, however, is tainted by his success a few weeks later when he steered a bill through the legislature banning Japanese sugar-beet farmers from Kansas. Such were the ironies of Kansas politics in the

444 Minnesota Avenue
Kansas City, Kansas
March 13, 1925

Mr. Ben S. Paulen
Governor of Kansas
Topeka, Kansas.

Dear Governor:-

The National Association for the Advancement of Colored People note the courageous stand that you took in the position of defeating the Klu Klux Klan Bill which came up in the House for passage.

The National Head at New York asked that the various Branches throughout the country extend to you our most hearty appreciation and thanks for this successful effort, which was championed in your speech in the House, on Thursday, when the bill was killed.

And we, from Kansas know how you are on these questions, without a doubt, and we stand ready to endorse and back you up in anything that you might desire in the future, for, we are satisfied that you are 100% American, and are willing to give every citizen in Kansas a chance, and that is all we ask of any officer of this country.

Very truly yours,

THE NATIONAL ASSOCIATION FOR THE ADVANCEMENT OF COLORED PEOPLE.

C. H. Major
PRESIDENT

Mamie Jones
SECRETARY

Rev. S. Montgomery
CHR. EXECUTIVE BOARD.

The NAACP thanked Governor Ben Paulen for opposing the Klan, although he would have likely signed Senate Bill 269. *Kansas Historical Society*.

1920s. Notwithstanding Hope's shortcomings, Klan options dwindled with the failure of the charter bill.[209]

The only way the Klan could win a charter in 1925 would be to appeal over the heads of the state supreme court by taking its case to the U.S. Supreme Court. It filed that March. Then in a triumph of hope over experience, the Klan filed another application for a charter in May 1925. Rejection was certain and arrived on July 1, 1925.[210]

In less than a year, whatever hopes the Klan held of attaining a legally recognized role in the state were dashed: the ouster suit, the reelection of Griffith and Ryan, the decision of the state supreme court, the defeat of the Klan bill and the rejection of the order's final charter application amounted to a wall of official resistance unlikely to fall. While some Klansmen may have held out hope for the U.S. Supreme Court's future decision on the ouster suit appeal, most members felt they had *one* final chance of gaining legal status in Kansas—victory in the 1926 general elections.[211]

The defeat of Attorney General Charles B. Griffith and Secretary of State Frank J. Ryan therefore became imperative to Klan survival. "The race for the Republican nomination for secretary of state has been the most spectacular…of any of the 1926 primary contests," the *Topeka Daily Capital* reported. Three Klan candidates entered the Republican primary for the post: Ewing Herbert, editor of the *Hiawatha (KS) Daily World*; Guy Swallow, former Topeka chief of police; and John A. Ryan, a Kansas City Democrat. "It appears," the *Kansas City Sun* reported, "that everybody except Frank Ryan has Klan support." Secretary of State Ryan was convinced that Governor Paulen had "injected the Kansas City Ryan into the race as a Klan ruse to make the nomination of Ewing Herbert possible." Ryan protested the Democrat's entry into the Republican race. The Kansas City Ryan appeared before the state canvassing board represented by attorney David F. Carson, a barrister with Klan ties. John A. was declared eligible for the primary, but Frank J. prevailed in Wyandotte County and elsewhere. In another blow to the Klan, William A. Smith, an assistant attorney general who worked on the ouster suit, defeated Klan-backed Max Anderson for the attorney general nomination.[212]

Undaunted, Wyandotte Klan No. 5 dutifully prepared for the 1926 campaign. Klan secretary C.W. Sayers placed an advertisement in the *Sun* pointing members to pro-KKK candidates, along with orders to get voters to the polls. No. 5's efforts paid off in the county races that summer, as twenty-one Klan Republican precinct committeemen were elected, seventeen of whom were political neophytes. One of the three Klan Democrats elected was also a first-time winner.[213]

The 1926 races with the specter of statewide Klan defeat and permanent ouster from the state gave the precinct elections a special urgency. Thus, "in several of the 199 precincts the fights for the job of precinct committeemen were some of the closest battles of the day," the *Kansan* reported. The precinct captains would elect the new chairman of the Republican County

100—Wyandotte County Court House, Kansas City, Kansas

Numerous Klansmen won public office in the county courthouse. Numerous other Klansmen tried. *Kansas City Public Library*.

Central Committee, and the Klan wanted him on its side. An intraparty war between Klan and non-Klan delegates was set to begin at the central committee's annual meeting on August 12.[214]

Klan attacks on political boss Thomas Bigger, alleged Missouri manservant and chairman of the committee, would now reach a peak. The Klan faction, headed by insurance man Earl D. Clark, nominated attorney David F. Carson for the post of county chairman. Bigger backed U. Grant Gates for the job. Gate's name *also* appears on the Wyandotte Klan No. 5 membership roster. Whether Bigger knew of Gate's Klan ties or not, the Clark candidate was the official Klan candidate. And whether Gates held political differences with his Klan comrades, had quit the hooded order or was conducting a clandestine political operation is equally unknown. Politics is strange. The records are silent.[215]

The rival wings battled for four hours, each side shouting that his man had the delegates to win the office. The disorder grew so "rioty," in the words of the *Kansas City Press*, that the sheriff was called to restore peace. During the tussle, Carson forces secretly collected the 102 committeemen signatures needed to win the election. The Bigger forces left in anger, and the Klan camp declared victory. Klansman C.W. Sayers called for adjournment, and the victors erupted in cheers.[216]

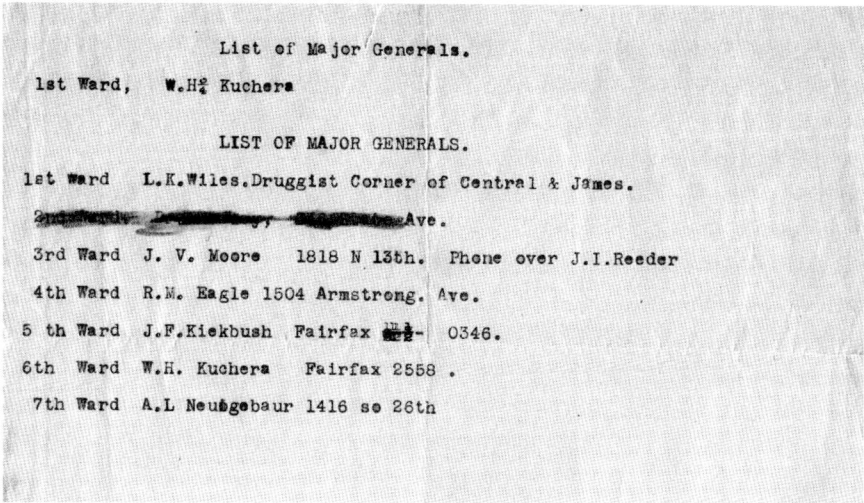

```
                    List of Major Generals.
    1st Ward,    W.H. Kuchera

                    LIST OF MAJOR GENERALS.
    1st Ward    L.K.Wiles.Druggist Corner of Central & James.
    2nd Ward                              Ave.
    3rd Ward    J. V. Moore    1818 N 13th.  Phone over J.I.Reeder
    4th Ward    R.M. Eagle 1504 Armstrong. Ave.
    5 th Ward   J.F.Kiekbush  Fairfax      0346.
    6th Ward    W.H. Kuchera   Fairfax 2558 .
    7th Ward    A.L Neubgebaur 1416 so 26th
```

The Klan reinstated councilmanic government, if only unofficially, when it arrived in the city. *Kansas Historical Society*.

Not only did Carson, with African American support, win the county chairmanship, but Klansman H.T. Barclay also was named secretary-treasurer. C.W. Sayers became chairman of the executive committee, which included Klansman D.M. Boddington as a member. The Klan's influence in Republican affairs was soon seen in the appointment of Barclay as Governor Paulen's chief of staff, an assignment arranged by Earl D. Clark.[217]

"Carson's election marks the downfall of the Thomas Bigger machine, which for more than sixteen years has been in control of local Republican politics," the *Kansan* noted. Bigger's reign had begun with the 1910 debut of commission-style government in Kansas City, Kansas. Viewed through the Klan's mask, commission government meant removing power from the neighborhoods and giving it to leaders elected "at large." At-large commissioners were believed to favor closer political and business ties with Kansas City, Missouri.[218]

Kansas City Klansmen further opposed commission government as undemocratic. One of their first actions upon entering the city in 1921 was to restore the old councilmanic ward system, at least unofficially, by the appointment of "Major Generals." Exalted Cyclops Burcham ordered the generals to "look after the moral and financial welfare of the wards." Like the ward heelers of old, the generals reported their observations and the complaints they received from the residents of their wards to Burcham. Potholes and bootleggers were common complaints. Burcham either referred the complaints to the city or kept them for action by the Klan.[219]

In January 1926, anti-commission groups began forming to re-instate councilmanic government officially. "In view of the fact that Kansas City is composed of a number of separate and distinct districts, each with their own individual identity, it is charged that the commission form of government is not truly representative," the *Sun* explained. Klansmen and prominent former Klansmen organized the Representative Government League. Klansman Lawrence E. Wilson was elected secretary. Former Klansmen Louis S. Harvey and E.N. Enright served the legal committee. Klansmen W.E. Brandenburg, John Bridges, Richard R. Fleck, W.J. Wright Jr., David Kepler Jr. and Dr. K.C. Haas were appointed to serve their respective wards' organizing committees. The campaign to reinstate the ward system failed despite Klan help.[220]

While boosting the councilmanic form of government, Klansmen at the same time led opposition to a countermeasure designed to improve "the evils of the commission system" with the adoption of the city manager plan. The innovation put power at the disposal of a non-elected city official, a terrifying prospect for Klansmen. But like the campaign to revert to the council, the measure to revolutionize the city's governing system failed.[221]

Notwithstanding Klan voter organization, precinct committee victories and party takeover, anti-Klan forces triumphed statewide in November 1926. Charter hopes vanished. Finally, in late February 1927, the U.S. Supreme Court declined to consider the Klan's ouster suit plea because it did not involve a federal law. The Klan had now failed at every level of appeal—political, administrative, legislative and judicial; local, state and federal. The hooded order was on an irreversible trajectory to irrelevance. But before the Invisible Empire completely faded from the state, there would be a great if ironic victory in Kansas City. Scandal paved the way.[222]

By 1925, Klan surrogate William W. Gordon, elected mayor over Harry B. Burton in 1923, was losing the confidence of city voters. Campaign promises to clean up the town remained only promises. Crime, booze and rumors of bribes dogged his administration. The city's hodgepodge layout and state-line escape hatch made effective law enforcement difficult. Mayor Gordon blamed part of the problem on the city's ethnic groups: "Croatians, Poles, Hungarians, Greeks, Mexicans, and Turks," who do not "speak the English language…and have been used to liquor in their own country." But it was soon clear the city's crime problem was worsened by a corrupt police force. The policemen were not only corrupt, it was charged, but they also were unfair. Bootleggers accused Kansas City policemen of arresting them only after pocketing their bribes. Chief of Police N.J. Wollard was obliged to resign when it was alleged that he took part in the shakedowns. Klan police officer Stanley Beatty was offered the chief's job but retained his police captaincy instead. Frank Wisdom, a non-Klansman, was finally appointed to replace Wollard.[223]

The police department scandal fueled more speculation about the integrity of Gordon's administration. By spring 1926, frustrated Kansas Citians were demanding an official probe of city conditions. Anti-Klan attorney general C.B. Griffith appointed the ubiquitous Louis S. Harvey as a special assistant attorney general to investigate the city. This seems an unlikely choice, but Harvey's reputation survived his Klan fling. Having a brother on the state supreme court probably did not hurt, either.

The Harvey Report was ready in June, but its contents were kept secret. The report detailed boundless graft in the awarding of municipal contracts and prohibition violations, the same two troubles that had forced the ouster of Mayor W.W. Rose in 1906 and led directly to the adoption of government by commission in 1909. Curiously, Griffith further delayed release of the report to the public. He instead began a series of raids on Kansas City speakeasies. Declaring the city a "cesspool and a stinking place," the attorney general outraged Kansas City citizens who wanted him banned from their town. A mass protest meeting, called to order by Klansman Richard R. Fleck, in his new capacity as president of the Parkwood Tax League, called for the immediate release of the Harvey Report. Griffith finally made the report public on September 3, 1926. He filed an ouster suit against Mayor Gordon the next day.[224]

The lines were drawn quickly, deeply and politically. Gordon accused Griffith of ignoring his pleas for law-enforcement aid earlier in the year. He heard nothing from the attorney general until Gordon sued W.D. Pratt, a political crony of Griffith, for the faulty construction of a settling basin. It was only then, Gordon charged, that Griffith began investigating conditions in Kansas City, which soon turned into a political operation to remove him from office. Pratt, like his friend Griffith, was linked to the *Kansas City Star*.[225]

Gordon's countercharges failed to save him, and he was suspended from office. His attorney, David F. Carson, argued, "The ouster suit against Mayor Gordon was instituted for no other reason than to protect Bill Pratt, Tom Bigger, and others….Gordon was ousted for no other reason than that he refused to look the other way." Louis S. Harvey was considered for interim mayor but lost the appointment to J.O. Emerson.[226]

Whatever the truth of the state's charges of law enforcement failure, or financial irregularities against Mayor Gordon, or Carson's charges of *Star*-inspired mischief, the conflict revealed the familiar alignment of forces: Klan and stand-pat politicians versus anti-Klan and *Star* progressives. The episode was glutted by men with current or former Klan ties. In addition to the involvement of Louis S. Harvey and David F. Carson, Klansmen D.H. Vance, A.L. Murphy, Charles Langford, Stanley Beatty and Charles Costello appeared among those filing affidavits in the case.[227]

So another scandal passed. But this time, the Klan would ensure that no so-called reform plagued the city before it returned to its senses. This time, there would be no surrogate candidates. This time, it would take the city for itself, and keep it.

7

"EVERYTHING THAT IS GOOD"

Judge Don Carlos McCombs of the city's Klan-dominated South City Court would be No. 5's man in the 1927 municipal elections. Born in 1880 in New Albany, Indiana, McCombs arrived in Kansas City at age eighteen. He settled in Armourdale and, like many young men there, found work in a packinghouse. But McCombs longed for more and hied off for Alaska in search of Klondike gold. The adventure failed to make him rich, but his ambitions survived the trip. He clerked for a grocer and bought the store from its owner, only to lose it all in the massive Kansas City flood of 1903. His backup plan saved him. The days behind the counter had been followed by nights behind a desk at the Kansas City School of Law. He graduated in 1907. By the next year, he was the assistant city attorney. Four years later, at age thirty-two, he became judge of the South City Court. McCombs stayed in Republican politics for the rest of his life.[228]

A popular justice, McCombs was known for fairness and a generous leniency in the courtroom. His role in the proceedings against the Gordon administration launched a boomlet for his candidacy. He agreed to run in February. He won the office in April. Armourdale, home to a boisterous Klan spirit, celebrated the victory with a holiday. The *Kansas City (KS) Weekly Press* reported, "Automobiles were in service, flying banners proclaiming the favorite candidates; there was said to be plenty of money in use in spite of the efforts of County Attorney Mellott, the police were very active for McCombs, lively scenes, good old days as of other times."[229]

Judge McCombs "was backed in his campaign by several large organizations, and organizations demand jobs," the *Kansan* warned. And by "organizations," the paper meant the Klan. Yes, McCombs owed the hooded order, but he knew better than to cloak his *entire* administration in a white robe. While he appointed Louis S. Harvey as city attorney, he replaced Klansman James P. Fox as police judge. Before naming an ally to the bench who likely belonged to the Klan, McCombs even considered former judge and Catholic Klan foe George H. West for the job. In 1928, McCombs named his former clerk, Klansman Bina S. Quick Jr., as secretary to Chief of Police William McMullen. The chief had ignored the Klan's call, but at least McCombs had a kluxer in McMullen's office. Klansman D.M. Boddington, streets commissioner, was also victorious in 1927. Boddington appointed Klansman Charles Langford as his clerk. Langford, Quick and Fox had served with McCombs on the South City court. Fox was apparently cut from the new regime, because he served under Mayor Emerson in the interim administration following Gordon's departure.[230]

McCombs's election fatally damaged the Bigger machine. Following the victory, Governor Paulen appointed Frank Thompson as judge of the South City court to fill McCombs's vacancy. A grateful Kansas City Republican thanked the governor: "I believe his [Thompson] appointment will… result in amalgamating all of the forces in this county, except those of Tom Bigger. I think it is high time that he be given the go-by and that it clearly be shown to him that we can get along without his service and assistance." The McCombs-Klan triumph was nearly total.[231]

The political victories of 1927 put the Klan at the very peak of Kansas City power. But peaks are unstable things when the earth moves beneath them. National scandals shook the Invisible Empire hard. The worst scandal entangled the powerful grand dragon of Indiana, D.C. Stephenson, when he forcibly intoxicated, raped and mauled a female acquaintance. She attempted suicide by drinking poison to escape Stephenson's depravity. He refused to take her to the hospital unless she agreed to marry him. Her refusals ended her life three weeks later when bite wounds inflicted by Stephenson turned into staph infections. Her body compromised beyond repair, the poison at last finished its job. Stephenson spent nearly thirty years in prison for the crime. Bitter at the loss of power, the former grand dragon exposed Klan malfeasance in hopes of winning parole. He stayed in prison, but his revelations further scandalized the embattled Invisible Empire.[232]

Klanfolk across the county fled the order like it was a burning theater as news of the scandals spread. Kansas felt the exodus. In April 1926,

Grand Dragon Charles H. McBrayer, Kansas' highest-ranking Klansman, offered former members clemency from past debts if they agreed to pay one-quarter membership dues ($1.25) and rejoin the order. Kansas City newspaper notices of Klan events also invited former members to reenlist in the Invisible Empire at a discount. No. 5 offered prizes to the Klan member who corralled the most recruits. By this time, practically anyone would do, even foreigners. The Klan in Kansas City welcomed the organization of an American Crusaders chapter in the city. The Crusaders were open to any white Protestant regardless of birthplace. While the Klan was officially closed to the foreign born, Wyandotte Klan No. 5 violated the rule several times, most notably in the case of the Scotsman David T. Cruden. In the event, they needed the help.[233]

Scandal was not the only thing driving Klan members from the klavern. The order's many successes in politics and other realms of interest threatened the necessity of the empire. Klansmen and Klanswomen needed something different from the hooded order if their most important needs had been met. The success of the white Protestant revival also lessened the need for the earlier muscular expressions of Klan power—the threats to minorities and public officials. The 1924 Immigration Act, eagerly embraced by Klanfolk as well as progressives such as the anti-Klan newspaperman William Allen White, stemmed the tide of non-Protestant immigration from Europe and, with it, fears of "alien" usurpations. The removal of a major problem was another reason to remove the white robe.[234]

The appointment of a Klan "Reclamation Officer" as the new exalted cyclops of Wyandotte Klan No. 5 in 1927 signaled more trouble; the local chapter needed rescue. With A.W. Murray's arrival from Klan headquarters in Washington, D.C., No. 5's activities shifted to lectures, "degree" work, dances, concerts and other social activities. Klan nights included "Overall and Apron" parties, "Tacky" parties and other gimmicks aimed at keeping the boys (and girls) in their hoods.[235]

The Klan in Kansas and throughout the nation was briefly reenergized by the candidacy of New York governor Al Smith as the Democratic presidential nominee in 1928. Smith personified several Klan hates. He was Catholic. He was Irish. He worked for an ethnic political machine. And he was a "wet"—an opponent of the nation's Eighteenth Amendment to the Constitution. Exalted Cyclops Murray and Grand Dragon McBrayer led a state fundraising drive to help defeat Smith, whom to no one's surprise they branded a "menace to American principles as he owes his allegiance to the pope, a foreign potentate."[236]

KNIGHTS OF THE KU KLUX KLAN, INC.

Atlanta, Ga.,_____192____

To All Faithful Klansmen, Greeting:

This is to Certify that Kl._____

was, on the_____day of_____192___, elevated to the degree of Knights Kamelia or K-Duo.

He should be so recognized and accepted as such upon presenting this Certificate accompanied by his dues card showing him to be in good standing in K-Uno.

Thus done and signed in the Imperial City of Atlanta, Commonwealth of Georgia, this_____day

of_____A. D. 192___, A. K._____.

Attest:

Imperial Kligrapp   Imperial Wizard

(Imperial Seal)

Issued and delivered in the Klavern of_____Klan No._____,

Realm of_____ _____.

Attest:

(Klan Seal)   Kligrapp   Exalted Cyclops

By 1928, the Klan stressed "degree" work and social activities over its previous political and night-riding emphases. *Author's collection.*

Knights of the Ku Klux Klan
and its Mission

By REALM LECTURER
Under Auspices of National Organization
KNIGHTS of the KU KLUX KLAN

Admit One   NOT TRANSFERABLE

Ticket to Klan lecture. *Author's collection.*

Governor Smith fared poorly against Republican Herbert Hoover in November, winning only eight states to Hoover's forty. But Smith fared better than Murray, who was arrested on fraud charges in St. Joseph, Missouri, for check forgery. Murray won four years in the Missouri State Penitentiary for his crimes. His wife and six Klan associates were arrested in December 1928 when they attempted to kidnap ("take him for a ride") Klansman Walter T. Ekel, whom they believed snitched out the exalted cyclops to the police. The abductors were apprehended by Kansas City police captain Stanley Beatty, also associated with the order.[237]

Scandals large and small were a factor in the retirement of Grand Dragon McBrayer, who lamented to his son that the wrong element had seized control of the Ku Klux Klan. The embarrassment weighed on the entire order. Public Klan events in Kansas City disappeared after the Murray debacle. No more picnics were mentioned in the local press. The city directory mirrors this demise. The Klan had its own meeting hall by 1925. Located in Fraternal Hall at 747 Minnesota Avenue, in the heart of the city's central business district, the order openly appeared in business directories under the Klan name. By 1929, the Klan moved its headquarters to 1720 Central Avenue, a building where several Klansmen kept business offices. South Kansas City, Armourdale and Argentine had produced many vocal and activist civic club and Klan leaders. Often at odds with the elites installed along Minnesota Avenue, south-side partisans like *Kansas City (KS) Republic* editor and publisher E.W. Wells undoubtedly understood the symbolic importance of the Klan's retreat from Minnesota Avenue.[238]

The KKK disappeared from the city guide in 1930. The last public sign of the order was in the summer of 1930 as Klan chapters from Kansas City, Olathe, Ottawa, Shawnee, Merriam, DeSoto, Edgerton, Overland Park and Lawrence, Kansas, gathered for a convention at the Bonner Springs Klan Hall. Portions of a diary shared with the author note Klan activity in Kansas City in the early 1930s, but the order had ceased to be a mass movement by then. The writer observed that the Kansas City chapter was down to 50 members. Only 3,500 Klansmen survived in the state. Rex Copp was elected exalted cyclops in 1933. He had been a member since 1922, when he joined the Klan at the Old Armory. Only a few well-known names from No. 5's early days mark the diary: John Zeller, Clarence Sayers, D.H. Burcham, John Werner and Dr. Warren Marshall. These true believers were still wearing the sheet a decade after joining the Invisible Empire.[239]

Following the election of Mayor McCombs and the downfall of A.W. Murray, Wyandotte Klan No. 5, Argentine Klan No. 90, Bonner Springs

Boyns Hall at the intersection of Eighteenth Street and Central Avenue housed Klan headquarters. The building still stands. *Author's collection.*

Klan No. 9 and Rosedale Klan No. 17 gradually faded from the county's stage. Their ultimate disappearance did not happen overnight. White, native-born Protestants simply moved on, their energies redirected to other concerns. Paul Taneyhill, the Armourdale druggist, is an example of the transient Klansman. In 1920, Taneyhill served as director of the Sixth Ward Civic Club. In 1921, he joined the Klan. Eventually becoming a Klan officer, Taneyhill led the delegation that donated $402 to Bethany Hospital. In July 1922, Taneyhill helped organize the dissident Knights of America and managed Harry Lillich's run for sheriff. Taneyhill was officially "banished" from the Atlanta-based Klan in October 1922, probably for his role in the Knights of America. In 1928, he appeared as a Republican precinct committeeman. His search for a viable means of civic progress carried on.[240]

William G. Bird's long public career was also a search for progress through various movements, political or otherwise. His first campaign came at age sixteen, when he organized his fellow newsboys for the election of Kansas City, Missouri mayor T.B. Bellune. Bird next apprenticed with a locksmith and became active in the labor movement. He joined the Knights of Labor, the same union that had so roiled Kansas City, Kansas business interests in the city's early history. Bird maintained his Knights membership through a brief flirtation with the new Peoples Party, better known as the Populists, and carried it back with him to the Republican Party enthusiasms of his youth. His appointment as state labor commissioner in 1894 made him a well-known political figure in Kansas City. Bird acknowledged that he was also a member of the anti-Catholic American Protective Association. He even called for the nomination of Kansas City's APA mayor Nat Barnes to replace Governor Morrill in the next election; this despite Morrill's appointment of Bird to his own prominent position. The duration of Bird's time with No. 5 is unknown. His name does not appear among either the activists or the dissidents. Bird remained a popular elected official throughout the Klan era of the 1920s, despite the order's controversial presence in the city.[241]

Dr. J. Wesley Faust, a prominent physician, had the shortest of Klan tenures. He attended one meeting and quit. Faust said the Klan failed to meet his idea of service and Americanism. Charles Costello, a police detective, testified that he was a member for thirty days. President Harry S Truman's dalliance with the Klan was equally brief. Truman joined the Klan out of political expediency. He quit on principle when he learned the Klan would not allow him to appoint Catholics to office. Justice Hugo Black joined the Klan on the grounds that it was the most progressive political organization in Alabama. Perhaps, but it also must have appealed to his searing anti-Catholicism, which he did his level best to embed in his legal opinions.[242]

Political resistance played a powerful role in driving the order from Kansas and Kansas City. Governor Henry J. Allen shared common prejudices with Kansas Klansmen, particularly his instinctive anti-Catholicism. Allen admittedly did not oppose the Klan on principle. He objected to its means (secrecy) and its objective (power). His resistance was predicated on his role as an elected leader. His response was one of defensive authority. Despite his lack of sympathy for the Klan's Catholic targets, Allen's commitment to removing the order from Kansas should not be understated. Along with Representative Clifford Hope, Henry Allen presented the Klan an insurmountable if imperfect obstacle in its drive to power in Kansas.[243]

Kansas City mayor Harry B. Burton opposed the Klan politically, too. After all, it was composed of his political enemies. But Burton brought a fervor to the battle against the Klan that other anti-Klan elites lacked. Unlike Allen, he worked publicly with Catholic leaders to fight the Klan. He opposed the hooded order on principle while acknowledging its members' commitment, however wrongheaded, to Kansas City's well-being. Burton's sense of empathy for both the Klansmen and their victims graced his role with moral authority. Burton ran for the Democratic nomination for governor in 1924. After losing, he moved to Iowa briefly before settling permanently in North Platte, Nebraska. There he remained active in Democratic politics. President Truman named him postmaster for his party labors. Formerly a Methodist and a Mason, in 1957, Burton became a Roman Catholic and a member of the Knights of Columbus. His former Klan enemies would have registered little surprise at the news.[244]

Despite their different styles, Burton and former governor Allen, Attorney General Charles B. Griffith and the state charter board led the state's war on the Klan to victory. Their resistance to the Klan was crucial to its defeat, but the resistance of Klan targets, particularly that of Roman Catholics, was just as critical to the victory.

The *Catholic Register*, the diocesan newspaper, reported, exposed and ridiculed Wyandotte Klan No. 5 with the sort of accuracy that can only have come from the inside of an organization. The *Register* either had a Klan informant or infiltrated the order. The paper broke the story of the Knights of America. The *Register* was also the first paper to report ongoing dissension in the Klan. In November 1922, for example, the *Register* "venture[d] the opinion that the Klan is dead." This report appeared a week before the state's ouster suit against the Klan was filed. On November 22, 1922, King Kleagle George T. McCarron ordered all Kansas Klansmen to resign from their chapter offices and forward all local records to him. The *Register's* fine-tuned ears caught news of these developments and concluded with relevant accuracy that the order was moribund in Kansas City, although, as in other instances, the Klan kept coming back to life after each breakup.[245]

But the *Register's* good fight strained the paper's resources:

> *We are grateful to the clergy and laity for the staunch support that has been accorded us not only in Kansas City but in all parts of the country. It cost us a large sum of money to carry on this fight but it was worth it. If you feel that we have done a service for you, the best way to tell us about it is to send us in an ad or an order for job printing. It is your paper—run for your especial benefit, religiously, socially, commercially and civically. It is your one line of offense and defense that can always be depended on to be in the thickest of the fight for right and justice. The stronger you make the* Register, *the easier it will be for you to live in peace and harmony with those who are ever ready to attack the defenseless.*[246]

OFFICE OF KING KLEAGLE
AND
GRAND DRAGON (TEMP)

November 22nd, 1922

Dated at K. C. Mo,

Send reply to P.O.Box 966

To all Exalted Cyclops
Klaliffs
Klokards
Kludds
•Kligrapps
Klabees
Kloragos
Klexters
Members of
Klokann
Night Hawks

My Dear Sirs   Realm of Kansas.
My dear Sirs:
          Owing to pending litigation in Kansas,
your are hereby directed to immediately resign from your
offices as Exalted Cyclops and Terrors of your organizations
forwarding your resignations in writing to this office at
once.

          For the same reason as stated above you men who are
Exalted Cyclops and Kligrapps are hereby directed to
immediately forward to this office all of your records.
Ship this by express money order package, addressing same
to this office, 218 Bryant Building, Kansas City, Mo.

          By records is meant, your charter, seal, dues card,
forms, roster of membership, record cards, lists of names,
correspondence, and any and all other matters such as are
listed.

                    I am,

                    Sincerely yours, ITSUB,

                    King Kleagle and Grand Dragon
                                             (Temp)

THE ACTION TAKEN ABOVE IS FOR THE BEST INTERESTS OF OUR
ORGANIZATION AND UPON THE ADVICE OF COUNSEL * SAY NOTHING
BUT "SAW WOOD"

King Kleagle George T. McCarron ordered Kansas Klansmen to turn in their records to the Klan in order to save them from state investigators. *Kansas Historical Society*.

James Malone of the Knights of Columbus also flummoxed Klan plans to dominate the city. Malone's vigor never waned as he campaigned against the circulation of the bogus oath, ludicrous stories of arsenals in church basements and the testimonies of "ex-nuns."

Malone's fellow Catholics worked with Jews and African Americans to defeat independent Klan candidate Harry Lillich in 1922. Black leaders, largely Republicans, carefully balanced party loyalty with anti-

Klan resistance. Their strategy was to maintain their share of power in the GOP even if it meant alliance with the Klan on specific political objectives. Kansas City African American Republicans like Thomas Kennedy, editor and publisher of the *Advocate*, pursued a realistic policy of accommodation on political matters but resisted overt Klan initiatives. For example, black Republicans were aligned with Klan Republicans during the shakeup surrounding L.H. Chapman's resignation in 1922, but they rejected or attempted to return Klan church donations made at the same time. Individual African Americans struck back at the Klan by refusing to yield to their demands to leave white neighborhoods. The bravery of Willis H. Summers to remain at 549 Greeley despite being surrounded by one hundred Klansmen showed the hooded order that the African American community would not easily surrender to its thuggery.[247]

African Americans leaders also opposed Klan plans to bring *The Birth of a Nation* to Kansas City. Non-Klan Kansas Republicans had kept the picture out of Kansas for eight years until Governor Davis, perhaps bowing to political realities of his own, let the movie be shown in 1923. "It seems to me," Klan newspaper editor Orrin B. Strong of Fort Scott, Kansas, reminded the governor, "that with all the interest there is under the subject, the heavy membership of an interested organization in this section of the state makes the subject one of particular political significance." Two

The Soldiers and Sailors Memorial hosted Klan minstrel shows and *The Birth of a Nation*. *Kansas City Public Library*.

years later, the issue returned. Wyandotte Klan No. 5 brought the film to Kansas City in December 1925 and won an injunction against those seeking to block its exhibition. The NAACP appealed to Governor Paulen, the Klan-endorsed candidate of the 1924 election, without effect. Members of the city's prominent African American organization, the Civic League, approached Attorney General Charles B. Griffith for aid. "Is there anything that you can do to prevent presentation, which can do no good: but which may do a great deal of harm? It is a great pity, that men can not find that— which better becomes their time and talent—than this needless appeal to prejudice." The appeal to Griffith also failed, and the movie played just as the Klan planned.[248]

The resistance of African Americans and other Klan targets, as well as the many Klan scandals, pushed Wyandotte Klan No. 5 from the city. The aftershocks of its active years, however, were to be felt for a quarter century thanks to the victory of Judge McCombs in the 1927 city elections.

From the start, there was suspicion over what the new administration might bring. The *Weekly Press* admonished its readers:

> *As Armourdale was quite unanimous for Don McCombs, all classes supporting him, his overwhelming election must not be wholly taken as a victory of the bootlegger, the punch board operator and the cigarette smoker. Many bitter disappointments will be devoured, after Mr. McCombs has been installed in office, for the lawbreaker will not receive as many favors as he expects. As mayor, Don McCombs will be put to the acid test and here's hoping he will succeed and he will succeed, if he pays some attention, if he pays more attention to the men who become rich; those who hold up their hands in holy horror at the pint flask and hide behind it and reap graft handling the business of the city.*[249]

The suspicion was still there at the time of his first run for reelection in 1931. Like his fellow Klansmen, McCombs's interpretation of the Republican party philosophy rejected the pro-Missouri "Greater Kansas City Agenda" favored by the city's larger commercial interests. The business class challenged him at the first opportunity, pitting soap plant executive Robert E. Crowley against the mayor. McCombs won by three thousand votes, the *exact* number of Christmas turkeys distributed by his workers four months hence. The paper thought it not a coincidence. Distrust would darken McCombs's reign like the long winter nights of his youthful Alaskan spree.[250]

IN THE DISTRICT COURT OF THE UNITED STATES FOR THE
DISTRICT OF KANSAS , IN AND FOR THE
FIRST DISTRICT.

C.F.Elerick,
          Plaintiff
    vs.   No._____
Harry Darby, et al,
          Defendants

RESTRAINING ORDER.

Now, upon this _____ day of December, this matter
being heard upon the petition of plaintiff, for a restraining order, directed to the defendants as hereinafter named,
and in the manner herein named, the Court finds upon consideration of said petition, that the same should be granted;

It is considered, and ordered that you, and each of
you as follows, to-wit: Harry Darby, Frank Strickland, Jr.,
and J.L.Otterman, being trustees of the Memorial Building
of Kansas City, Kansas and N.W.Gordon, mayor of Kansas
City, Kansas; and Arthur Strickland, F. LeRoy Cook, Henry
Scheible, and C.D. Darnall, city commissioners of the city
of Kansas City, Kansas; and F.M. Wisdom, chief of police of
Kansas City, Kansas; and Harry Hayward, county attorney of
Wyandotte County, Kansas; and Daniel (Bob) Mayer, sheriff of
Wyandotte County, Kansas; and Charles B.Griffith, attorney
general of the State of Kansas; and their agents, servants,
employees, and deputies, and each of them, be and they are
hereby restrained and enjoined from in any manner interfering with, preventing, or attempting to prevent, the exhibition of the moving picture " Birth of a Nation " in the Memorial Building in Kansas City, Kansas; until further order of
this Court; and they are further directed to appear before

The Ku Klux Klan filed a restraining order against parties attempting to block the exhibition of *The Birth of a Nation* in 1925. *Eisenhower Presidential Library.*

He ruled Kansas City for twenty years by building a bipartisan political machine made from vestiges of Wyandotte Klan No. 5. Represented by Klansman J. Earl Thomas, Democrats traded votes for patronage while the city was able to garner more aid from the permanently GOP state legislature by keeping a Republican mayor in office. The halting of new annexation until 1956 successfully blocked the creation of new county commission seats, a canny political move by McCombs that reduced the possibility of Democratic rivals emerging from the suburbs. The maneuver also staved off insurgent Democratic challenges to Judge Thomas, who occupied the bench in the city's police court thanks to his appointment by McCombs.[251]

McCombs's tenure brought the warnings of the *Weekly Press* to life. His administration, a local history records, "has been referred to as 'unprogressive,' a description that some might say is overly generous." Civic neglect was the theme of the McCombs era, said critics. The city's power plant was badly mismanaged. In the 1940s, 40 percent of Kansas City

SOLDIERS & SAILORS MEMORIAL-- MONEYS RECEIVED.

1925		
May 8, E.A.Schnock, Donation,		$300.00
" 26, Shrine Rent		75.00
" 26, American Legion-Rent		75.00
June 1, American Legion "		90.00
" 22, do.		75.00
July 2, "		50.00
" 6, Concession 6/26 7/3		47.30
" 2, (Board of Education)		75.00
" 14, American Legion-Tunney-		100.00
" 14, Eastern Star		225.00
Aug. 7, Cudahy Packing Co.		100.00
" 7, American Legion		150.00
" 7, Concessions,Greb fgt.		26.75
" 31, Colored Shrine		50.00
Sept.4, McCue Dance- Rent		35.00
" 5, Colored Shrine-Balance		75.00
" 8, Concessions,J.Rivers		
fight.		32.85
" 12, Deposit-Amer.Legion		150.00
" 25, Shrine- Colored Bal.		75.00
" 25, Mercantile Bureau		
(Merchants)		225.00
" 25, Concessions		3.95
" 28, " Cudahy Athletic		2.40
Oct.12, Merchants Fashion Show		31.20
" 13, Concessions, Industrial		
Show		54.70
" 15, Fight, Oct. 13, 1925		150.00
" 26, Civic Federation		
advance payment		5.00
" 24.00 Concessions-Boy Scouts-		4.30
10/24 Check of G.M.Harmon not		
cashed		17.60
Oct.27,St.Margarets Hosp.Ben.		75.00
Nov. 3, Concessions- Food show		72.55
" 3, Cudahy Athletic Club		100.00
" 3, Brotherhood Athletic-		
Advance Payment		10.00
" 9, Theta Chapter-Music.		20.00
Aug.31, Cash for Concessions		2.60
Nov. 7, St.Thomas B.B.Club		75.00
" 10, U.P.Ry.Athletic Club		30.00
" 12, Brotherhood Ath.Club		11.00
" 12, Cash " " "		39.00
" 4, Concessions-St.Thomas,		12.60
" 16, Brotherhood Athletic		17.30
" 16, Balance of rent "		90.00
" 21, Built Ring Bro. "		10.00
" 21, J.Fry pd.Bal on Rent		45.00
" 21, Concessions W.B.Dance		2.75
" 21, " on Firemen's Ball		20.05
" 23, Payment,Birth of Na.		10.00
" 27, Concessions-Police Ball		25.10
" 27, Colored Clubs- rent		20.00
" 30, Rent, Theta Chapter		20.00
Dec. 2, A.Peel- Hospital Rent		10.00
" 2, 5th annual food show		300.00
" 9, Brotherhood Athletic		150.00
" 9, Amer.Legion-Erecting		
Ring		10.00
" 9, Paragonian Club Ring		5.00
" 9, Grocery Show		24.20
" 15, C.W.Sayers .KKK		215.00
" 15, Concessions KKK		6.85
" 15, " Poultry Show		.30
" 21, Concessions, K.K.K.		38.05
" 26, Brotherhood Athletic		150.00
" 28, Shriners Party 12/22		75.00
" 28, Birth of Nation		12.50
" 28, Heissler -Brother.Ath.		19.85
" 28, State Teachers Convention		
		300.00
" 31, Rent- Ku Klux Klan		216.50
		4442.25

1926		
Jan. 4, Scottish Rite Dance		
Concessions-		21.10
" 4, Poultry Show		
rent		60.00
" 4, American Legion		52.50
" 5, Cudahy Ath.		
concessions		16.10
Agnes Peele Check		
never cleared		10.00
		4601.95

Approved

Records from the Soldiers and Sailors Memorial document revenue from Ku Klux Klan rentals and *The Birth of a Nation. Eisenhower Presidential Library.*

residences still had poor sewer service. Parks and swimming pools decayed. The State Board of Health closed six pools during McCombs's tenure. More dramatically, Kansas City's population decreased under the machine for the first time in the city's history. And if the McCombs machine rejected the alien forces of the *Star*, it embraced its own foreign entanglements, as the mayor was rumored to be nothing more than a local agent of Missouri (and Irish Catholic) political boss Tom Pendergast, as well as a glad hand to bootleggers and gamblers.[252]

By 1946, McCombs, now in his late sixties, decided to retire from public life. Sensing the opportunity for change, idealistic World War II veterans, some of whom were the sons of earlier Klan opponents, began organizing the city for reform. To remedy the neglect of the McCombs years, they formed the "Citizens Committee for City Manager Government." The mayor's forces countered with the "Citizens Committee for the Retention of Representative Government." Former Klansman and county attorney Justus N. Baird campaigned against the veterans' proposal in an echo of the earlier anti–city commission arguments of Klan members. "Progress can only be made where there is a scattering of power, rather than the concentration of power in an individual," Baird warned.[253]

Once again, the Klan, or remnants thereof, helped to prevent a post-scandal reform as the city-manager measure failed by a two-to-one margin.

Kansas City's Main Street during the reign of Klan mayor Don C. McCombs. *Kansas City Public Library*.

The power of the mayor's office intact, McCombs's forces met to pick his successor. Judge Thomas and former Klansmen Eli Dahlin, Stanley Beatty and E.W. Wells were among the group that secretly tapped Judge Clark E. Tucker to replace McCombs. Tucker won the election and retained Thomas as police judge. Thomas, like Mayor McCombs, was a graduate of the Kansas City School of Law. He even visited the White House in 1949 to reminisce with famous classmate Harry S Truman.[254]

The No. 5 machine stalled in January 1952, when the attorney general began investigating Judge Thomas's office. Secret tapes revealed that the judge sold tips of impending raids to bootleggers and gamblers and then squeezed them for political contributions. (The tapes also recorded the amorous exertions of the judge and his secretary.) Thomas was additionally accused of helping civil service applicants cheat on exams. The scandal made national news when city detectives loyal to the judge traded gunfire with private detectives removing a listening device from Thomas's office. The intruders were working for the state attorney general. Confronted with the mass of evidence collected by the attorney general's agents. Thomas resigned, along with Lieutenant Jack Stewart of the police raid squad. Stewart was also a former member of Wyandotte Klan No. 5.[255]

Judge Thomas never got his day in court. He died six months after the shootout on a trip to Texas. A stroke took his patron McCombs in 1951. With their deaths and the defeat of Mayor Tucker by Republican Paul Mitchum in April 1955, Kansas City's Klan era was finally over.

Despite Wyandotte Klan No. 5's earnest rhetoric about representing "everything that is good and clean, morally, righteously, and politically," the whole enterprise had been rotten from the start. Modern pluralistic societies cannot revert to an idealized state built around a single ethnic or cultural identity without conflict. Joining reactionary crusades to force the restoration of a class or a race to power leads otherwise normal people to abnormal actions.

Normal Kansas Citians donned the Klan robe and committed many acts surely later regretted. Wyandotte Klan No. 5 members reportedly clashed with Mexican parents over their children attending white schools. Although the Klan managed to avoid additional bloodshed—at least, none was reported—the order's leadership advocated its use; plans were readied for an operation to punish the school superintendent. No such debate attended the use of intimidation and terrorism. Normal Kansas Citians employed both tactics widely. They wielded the specter of their presence to threaten African American homeowners, forced removal of the Argentine High School dancing instructor and prevented the Catholic city engineer from becoming Kansas City Water and Light Commissioner. Normal Kansas Citians elected to public office utilized its power to enforce white Protestant cultural norms and values when they waged war on Sunday grocers and removed satiric novels from library shelves. These normal folks assumed powers reserved for government when they acted as a national spy service and police intelligence unit, hired private liquor investigators and appointed major generals to run the city's wards.

The history of the Ku Klux Klan in Kansas City, Kansas, is an ironic and cautionary tale of how embracing the hollow solidarity of a presumed superiority damaged the very thing it was trying to protect—its city.

A GLOSSARY OF KLANSPEAK

Exalted Cyclops	President
Grand Dragon	State President
Klaliff	Vice-President
Klokard	Lecturer
Kludd	Chaplain
Kligrapp	Secretary
Klabee	Treasurer
Kladd	Ritual Conductor
Kleagle	Salesman/Organizer
King Kleagle	District Manager/Salesman
Klarago	Inner Guard
Klavern	Chapter and Meeting Place
Klexter	Outer Guard
Klokan	Investigator
Klokann (plural)	Board of Investigators
Nighthawk	Charge of Candidates

Another commonly used phrase was *to klux*. That is, to organize a city or institution for the Ku Klux Klan. For example, "City hall was thoroughly kluxed."

Kluxer	Klan member
Kluxers (plural)	Klan members

The kluxers were also a secret night-riding faction within Wyandotte Klan No. 5. The Ku Klux Klan is also referred to in this book as the "hooded order" and the "Invisible Empire." Wyandotte Klan No. 5 is also referred to as No. 5. *Klanfolk* includes the entire community of men, women and children associated with the hooded order.

Appendix A
KLAN POLITICAL CANDIDATES, 1921–1930

(Asterisk denotes winner in primary and/or general election.
Names are listed in the order of their appearance in newspaper articles.)

1921 (INCLUDES PRIMARY AND GENERAL)

Mayor: D.H. Burcham
Commissioner of Waterworks and Street Lighting: E.J. Coleman

1922

Primary

County Clerk: William Beggs (R)*
Register of Deeds: U.G. Gates (R)*
County Attorney: Justus N. Baird (R)*; E.A. Enright (R)
Sheriff: David M. Kepler, Jr. (R), Harry Lillich (R), T.A. Powell (D), George
   W. Chess (D)
Coroner: J.W. Hayward (R)*
County Assessor: William G. Bird (R), J.M. Joslin (R)*
Marshal, City Court, First District: Charles Langford (R)*, A.E. Butcher (R)

Judge, City Court, Second District: Don C. McCombs (R)*
Clerk, City Court, Second District: Bina S. Quick Jr. (R)*, Roy Seigmund (R)
Quindaro Township Trustee: F.H. Morasch (R)
Shawnee Township Trustee: David Espenlaub

General

County Clerk: William Beggs (R)*
Register of Deeds: U.G. Gates (R)
County Attorney: Justus N. Baird (R)*
Sheriff: Harry Lillich (I)
Coroner: J.W. Hayward (R)*
County Assessor: J.M. Joslin (R)*
Marshal, City Court, First District: Charles Langford (R)*
Judge, City Court, Second District: Don C. McCombs (R)*
Marshal, City Court, First District: Charles E. Pointer (R)*
Clerk, City Court, Second District: Bina S. Quick Jr. (R)*

1923

Municipal Primary and General

Mayor: T.W. Hadley
Commissioner of Parks and Public Property: E.E. Stockdale, C.F. Higgins
Board of Education (four-year term): Dr. K.C. Haas
Board of Education (two-year term): D.H. Burcham, Bert R. Collins,
    George W. Durham*, L.E. Wilson

1924

Primary

Attorney General: Justus N. Baird (R)
County Clerk: William Beggs (R)*, Bina S. Quick Jr. (R)

County Attorney: Harry Hayward (R)*
Sheriff: Harry Lillich (R)
State Representative: D.H. Burcham (R), E.A. Enright (R)
County Commissioner, First: R.M. Eagle (R)*
County Commissioner, Second: David Espenlaub (R)*

General

County Clerk: William Beggs (R)*
County Attorney: Harry Hayward (R)*
Coroner: J.W. Hayward (R)*
County Commissioner [unknown] (R)*

1925

Municipal Primary and General

Commissioner of Water and Light: H.T. Barclay, J.M. Joslin
Commissioner of Parks and Public Property: W.J. Wright Jr., Ralph
    Daughden
Board of Education (four-year term): George W. Durham, D.M.
    Boddington*

1926

Primary

Judge, District Court Twenty-Ninth District, Fourth Division (regular
    term): L.S. Harvey (D)*
Representative, Eighth District: W.E. Brandenburg (D)*
Representative, Ninth District: Lester Gilmore (R)*
County Clerk: William Beggs (R)*
County Attorney: Harry Hayward (R)*
County Treasurer: William G. Bird (R)*

Sheriff: Stanley Beatty (R), Charles F. Langford (R), Harry Lillich (R), N.V. Reichenecker (R)

Coroner: J.W. Hayward

Public Administrator: J. Earl Thomas (D)*

Marshal, City Court, First District: Charles E. Pointer (R)*

Clerk, City Court, First District: Bina S. Quick Jr. (R)*

Judge, City Court, Second District: Don C. McCombs (R)*

General

Representative, Eighth District: W.E. Brandenburg (D)

Representative, Ninth District: Lester Gilmore (R)*

County Clerk: William Beggs (R)*

County Treasurer: William G. Bird (R)*

Country Attorney: Harry Hayward (R)

Clerk of District Court: Walter F. Mathis (R)*

Public Administrator: J. Earl Thomas

Marshal of City Court: David Kepler Jr. (R)*

Judge of City Court, Second District: Don C. McCombs (R)*

1927

Municipal Primary and General

Mayor: Don C. McCombs *

Commissioner of Finance and Revenue: W.E. Brandenburg

Commissioner of Streets and Public Improvements: D.M. Boddington*

Board of Education: Bert R. Collins

1928

Primary

Country Clerk: William Beggs (R)*
County Treasurer: William G. Bird (R)
County Attorney: Justus N. Baird (R), J. Earl Thomas (D)*
Coroner: J.W. Hayward (R)
County Assessor: R.M. Eagle (R)
Clerk, District Court: Walther F. Mathis (R)*
County Commissioner, First District: Frank Werner (R)*
County Commissioner, Third District: David Espenlaub (R)*, A.L.
    McCallum (R)
Marshal, City Court: David Kepler Jr. (R)*

General

County Clerk: William Beggs (R)*
County Attorney: J. Earl Thomas (D)
Clerk, District Court: Walter F. Mathis (R)*
Commissioner, First District: Frank Werner (R)*
Commissioner, Third District: David Espenlaub (R)*

1929

Municipal Primary and General

Board of Public Utilities: Tom Baird, L.J. Canfield, E.J. Coleman, B.R.
    Collins, David Gerber, Theodore L. Grindel, William G. Morse, J.C.
    Murray, A.L. McCallum, B.A. Spake, Henry E. Stone, Harry M.
    Swartz, J. Earl Thomas, Lawrence E. Wilson

1930

Primary

State Auditor: Clyde Latchem (R)
Representative, Seventh District: David Ben Gerber (R)
County Clerk: William Beggs (R)*
Country Treasurer: William G. Bird (R)
Sheriff: A.E. Butcher (R), Eli Dahlin (R)
Clerk, District Court: Walther F. Mathis (R)*, William G. Morse (D)*
Commissioner, Second District: O.S. Clark (R), R.B. Eagle (R)
Quindaro Township Justice of the Peace: J.W. Gill (R)
Qunidaro Township Constable: S.A. Divilbiss (R)
Quindaro Township Trustee: Everett Dillon (R)
Justice of the Supreme Court: L.S. Harvey (D)*

General

County Clerk: William Beggs (R)*
Clerk of District Court: Walter F. Mathis (R)*
Justice of the Supreme Court: L.S. Harvey (D)
Precinct Committee Captains

Klan political action grew throughout the decade, especially at the neighborhood level, where the precinct captains crucial to the order's political takeover of the city were elected. The seriousness of No. 5's campaign to capture these seats is seen in the 500 percent increase of Klan precinct committeemen elected from 1922 to 1928.

In 1922, there were seven Klan precinct committeemen (four Republicans and three Democrats); 1924: twenty-six Klan precinct committeemen (fifteen Republicans and eleven Democrats); 1926: twenty-five Klan precinct committeemen (twenty-two Republicans and three Democrats); and 1928: thirty-one Klan precinct committeemen (twenty-eight Republicans and three Democrats).

In 1930, there was a marked decline that parallels the local and national decline of the order. Only thirteen known Klansmen served as precinct committeemen at the end of the decade (twelve Republicans and one Democrat).

All races combined, the Ku Klux Klan in Kansas City, Kansas, won 130 democratically elected offices.

WYANDOTTE KLAN NO. 5 MEMBERSHIP ROSTER AND OCCUPATIONAL STATUS COMPARISON

The names come from four sources: The Ku Klux Klan membership list in the papers of Governor Henry J. Allen at the Library of Congress, the *Catholic Register* newspaper, the *Plaintiff's Abstract* to the Kansas ouster suit against the KKK and the *Kansas City Kansan* newspapers. The author has resisted the temptation to include the names of men who were *likely* members of the Klan in the narrative. The names were not included if there was any doubt of their membership.

Ackerman, F.B.
Adams, J.A.
Adams, Ray F.
Adams, V.C.
Aifers, Chas. G.
Akens, Homer T.
Akerstrom, G.G.
Albright, Wm. A.
Aldridge, R.G. AL
Alford, Matthew
Allen, Don C.
Allen, Harry W.
Alles, G.E.
Allin, J.M.

Allison, Geo. F.
Allsups, W.W.
Allvine, Fred C.
Alter, C.
Anders, Clark
Anders, Don B.
Anderson, Edwin H.
Anderson, E.F.
Anderson, E.H.
Anderson, Ernest H.
Anderson, Helmer
Arends, W.B.
Ash, T.R.
Asher, Roy

Asher, Worthy
Atherton, H.F.
Atkinson, L.B.
Atwood, Carl F.
Auguston, O.F.
Austin, Wm. T.J.
Babel, Roy D.
Bagley, Fenton
Baies, Chas. L.
Bailey, E.H.
Bailey, Logan
Baird, Justus N.
Baird, T.
Baker, E.S.

Baker, H.
Baker, Wm. A.
Ball, C.H.
Bangs, Carl F.
Bannister, H.
Bantleon, C.A.
Barackman, C.F.
Barber, P.H.
Barber, R.P.
Barclay, H.T.
Barclay, J.F.
Barner, A.E.
Barnes, C.R.
Barnes, Frank
Barnes, Geo. N.
Barnet, E.G.
Barnett, S.H.
Barnham, Geo. F.
Barnhart, Jas. A.
Barns, Wm. C.
Barshfield, C.P.
Barshfield, William
Barthowley, S.
Bartlett, R.H.
Bates, ?
Bates, Norman
Batten, E.D.
Baxter, J.H.
Beatty, Stanley
Beck, Chas.
Beeler, C.V.
Beets, N.E.
Beggs, William "Billy"
Behrens, A.O.
Bemell, Walter
Bence, L.B.
Bennett, B.E.
Benson, G.R.
Benthine, A.H.

Berhard, W.C.
Bernitz, C.C.
Berry, N.B.
Biddle, ?
Bidwell, Earl M.
Bidwell, Geo. H.
Bidwell, M.H.
Billington, J.D.
Bird, Wm. G.
Birdsong, Virgil
Bishop, Rob.
Bishop, Wm. E.
Black, Leroy E.
Black, Wm. F.
Blanchard, Chas. G.
Bloom, A.J.
Blum, Geo. B.
Boatmen, M.E.
Boddington, D.D.M.
Boddington, G.M.
Boeck, L.W.
Bogue, Wm. F.
Bolton, P.C.
Booth, M.L.
Borchardt, H.R.
Boreges, Clifford
  (Clifred)
Borges, Milt
Boswell, Henry T.
Boutwell, F.W.
Bowden, H.T.
Bowling, J.A.
Bowling, Vernon G.
Bowman, Robt. T.
Boyce, N.V.
Boyer, ?
Boyer, Earl E.
Bracken, W.C.
Bradbury, G.A.

Bradbury, Howard
Bradbury, J.H.
Bradshaw, H.D.
Bratton, Paul
Bray, M.
Brelsford, A.C.
Brenner, H.P.
Bressler, C.W.
Bridges, John L.
Bridges, O.S.
Bridgewater, J.R.
Broomfield, John B.
Brose, C.H.
Brown, A.E.
Brown, C.E.
Brown, Elmer L.
Brown, Frank D.
Brown, H.J.
Brown, H.R.
Brown, J.B.
Brown, S.E.
Brown, W.S.
Brown, William S.
Bruce, Melvin
Brunk, S.C.
Buchanan, L.R.
Buckland, W.H.
Buckley, John F.
Bullock, H.A.
Burcham, D.H.
Burge, Homer E.
Burns, Chas. E.
Burns, Fred L.
Burr, Claude L.
Busby, R.B.
Butcher, A.E.
Butte, John J.
Buttrain, L.I.
Butts, R.L.

Butts, Robt. L.
Bybee, Robt. A.
Caldwell, Chas. C.
Caldwell, Wm. W.
Callahan, Wm. A.
Calver, Wm. C.
Calvin, Harry A.
Calvins, H.J.
Cameron, Ralph C.
Campbell, C.C.
Campbell, J.T.
Canfield, L.J.
Cantrell, H.C.
Capler, Jeff D.
Capts, L.B.
Carl, D.H.
Carmitchel, R.E.
Carr, Bentley B.
Carter, Alva H.
Carthers, F.G.
Cartmill, Bruce E.
Carver, G.T.
Carver, Lorenzo F.
Cassidy, Thos. E.
Cassity, A.L.
Cater, Harry L.
Chamberlain, D.P.
Chandler, M.L.
Cheatwood, B.E.
Cherington, Roy
Chess, Geo. W.
Chester, Wm. H.
Christiansen, A.L.
Christiansen, Norman
Clark, B.W.
Clark, F.C.
Clark, O.S.
Claughley, Jos. T.
Claxton, John

Clayton, A.W.
Clayton, Reeves G.A
Clemens, S.L.
Clockley, Jos.
Coates, A.S.
Coffman, R.N.
Cole, Frank R.
Cole, Horace B.
Coleman, E.J.
Collar, L.H.
Collins, B.R.
Conklin, D.H.
Connell, Edwin L,
Connelly, W.E.
Connoy, Rowland
Conradson, Max
Cook, R.L.
Cooley, E.N.
Cooper, M.L.
Cooper, M.O.
Copeland, H.E.
Copp, Rex
Cornelius, J.E
Costello, C.E.
Coy, Jas. H.
Craft, L.W.
Craggs, W.E.
Craig, Lloyd
Crail, Edgar S.
Crawford, A.L.
Crawford, C.C.
Crawford, L.A.
Creed, Charles C.
Crippen, John L.
Critchfield, W.W.
Crockett, Kelley D.
Croll, ?
Croll, ?
Croll, Forrest B.

Croll, John L.
Cronkhite, L.E.
Cross, W.P.
Crow, Wesley
Croy, F.M.
Crum, Thos. H.
Crutchfield, W.M.
Culp, Frank,
Culver, G.J.
Culver, Ray C.
Curtis, J.D.
Dahlin, Ele (Eli)
Dale, Dick B.
Dallas, H.H.
Daniels, Chas. O.
Daughden, Ralph
Davidson, D.D.
Davidson, E.S.
Davidson, J.J.
Davis, G.R.
Davis, L.C.
Dehis, Hy. H.
Deitrick, W.H.
Dennett, C.W.
Dennett, Robt. W.
Denney, M.E.
Dennis, Max
Deugel, Harry E.
Deugel, L.H.
Dewey, B.M.
Diemer, G.G.
Dillon, E.
Diltz, P.B.
Dimick, P.E.
Dinwiddle, Frank
Dixon, Mitchell
Dolph, E.S.
Dolzer, W.M.
Dougal, W.T.

Doughterty, S.A.
Doughty, J.L.
Draper, Issacs A.
Drenner, John V.
Drier, Louis A.
Drysdale, L.R.
Duckworth, B.T.
Duffendack, F.L.
Duvall, John T.
Eagle, R.B.
Eagle, R.M
Earl, Wm. J.
Easley, John L.
Edwards, A.F.
Edwards, C.B.
Ekel, Walter
Ellegard, E.T.
Ellerman, Geo. C.
Ellington, C.A.
Elliott, C.J.
Ellis, J.H.
Ellis, Shelby
Ellis, W.N.
Ellison, W.E.
Ellsworth, W.E.
Englemore, Otto H.
English, Geo. B.
Enright, E.A.
Espenlaub, D.F.
Etter, J.E.
Evans, Roy C.
Evans, T.R.
Evary, Frank
Everett, L.F.
Everly, W.F.
Eversole, Paul K.
Fabiaus (Fabian?), H.W.
Fahl, Wm. A.
Fairchild, L.J.

Fairweather, John
Farrar, Robt. C.
Farrow, E.H.
Faus, A.A.
Fausch, L.F.
Faust, Dr. J.W.
Faust, Homer F.
Faust, Otto C.
Fawks, E.A.
Feagles, G.Z.
Fee, John T.
Feenthop, H.L.
Ferguson, W.G.
Ferrell, J.M.
Fields, Robt. H.
Fillings, J.L.
Fimes, Ernest F.
Fimreck, Chas. R.
Fink, K.W.
Fisher, J.T.
Fisher, W.J.
Flanders, Chester
Fleck, Richard R.
Fleenor, John W.
Fleetwood, Preston
Fleming, B.G.
Fleming, N.J.
Fletcher, C.C.
Flora, Jefferson H.
Flower, C.E.
Forrester, R.
Forsberg, C.W.
Foster, Guy A.
Fouts, Claud
Fowler, Arthur A.
Fox, Jas. P.
Frank, Chas. W.
Frank, R.A.
Fuchs, Fred W.

Fuller, Albert C.
Fuller, H.V.
Fuller, John M.
Fulton, Jas. A.
Fultz, Guy
Furgason, Bert
Gable, Chas. W.
Gable, J.J.
Gagel, A.J.
Gallehugh, G.F.
Gamber, A.L.
Gardner, John E.
Garrett, A. Brenner
Garrett, Henry B.
Garrett, John W.
Garrison, A.
Gaskill, Clem
Gassler, C.E.
Gates, M.W.
Gates, U. Grant
Gee, Wm. W.
Geiger, C.F.
Gelvin, Guy N.
George Jr., E.F.
Gerber, D.B.
Ghrist, D.A.
Gibbs, C.F.
Gibson, W.M.
Gilbert, G.W.
Gill, John W.
Gillespie, S.B.
Gillett, B.B.
Gillspie, T.L.
Gilmore, Artie T.
Gilmore, Lester
Gles, Chas. A.
Godfrey, J.B.
Godfrey, S.K.
Goff, J.A.

Goings, John W.
Good, Arthur L.
Goodman, E.Y.
Gordon, J. Riley
Gorsage, Dean
Gorsuch, H.F.
Gottman, E.E.
Grable, Anson V.
Gray, H.B.
Gray, Leroy P.
Gray, Wm. G.
Graybill, J.D.
Green, O.Z.
Gresch, C.A.
Griffin, Frank
Griffith, J.F.
Grindel, Theo.
Grinter, R.H.
Gripen, F.H.
Groves, E.C.
Grubb, John C.
Grueninger, John J.
Grueninger, W.H.
Gruner, H.A.
Guimm, A.A.
Guinn, L.K.
Gunn, Devoy
Guy, W.A.
Haas, Dr. K.C.
Haberlein, F.A.
Hadley, Theo. Walter
Hadley, Dr.
Hafeman, W.J.
Hagedorn, O.E.
Hahn, Wm. E.
Hale, Jas. F.
Hall, Art F.
Halloway, J.L.
Hamil, J.A.

Hamilton, J.L.
Handwerk, John
Hanes, C.F.
Hanes, Oscar B.
Harber, L.N.
Hardine, Benj.
Hardwick, O.L.
Harman, E.G.
Harman, Lee
Harper, Harvey
Harper, R.L.
Harpst, F.W.
Harrier, Wm. A.
Harrington, W.P.
Harris, Frank L.
Harris, L.H.
Harris, Matt A.
Hart (?), Earl
Hartman, D.T.
Hartnett, John
Hartung, H.C.
Hartweg, G.A.
Harvey, L.S.
Hastings, C.E.
Hastings, W.C.
Hatfield, Thos.
Hattley, R.J.
Hattley, T.C.
Haug, Chas. A.
Haug, E.P.
Havely, S.R.
Hawkey, Cyrus T.
Hayes, Edw. E.
Haynes, E.O.
Hayward, Harry
Hayward, J. Wm.
Hedge, Frank E.
Hedrick, C.C.
Hedrick, Paul

Hedricks, Clarence
Hedstrom, A.G.
Heeter, J.B.
Heeter, Vann
Heidenreich, J.P.
Hem, John T.
Hemphill, F.J.
Hempstead, C.E.
Hempstead, Fred
Henry, R.L.
Henry, R.W.
Henry, W.O.
Hergen (?), Arthur O.
Hershey, John R.
Hickman, M.L.
Hickock, Frank R.
Hickock, F.E.
Hicks, W.F.
Higgins, C.F.
Higman, R.R.
Hignian, J.C.
Hills, L.D.
Hilton, J.H.
Hoagland, Fred W.
Hobbs, M.C.
Hoch, Merle K.
Hock, G.E.
Hodges, W.W.
Holcomb, W.T.
Holden, R.E.
Holitza, Harry H.
Hollquist, Edward
Hollquist, E.G.
Hollquist, Hugo F.
Holmes, B.F.
Holtzclaw, R.
Holyfield, J.H.
Hopkins, C.C.
Hopkins, J. Calvin

Hopkins, "Lefty"
Horley, John T.
Hubbard, Robt. C.
Huff, L.B.
Hulburd, Dwight G.
Hull, G.W.
Hunt, J.C.
Hunt, Jas.
Hunter, C.R.
Hutchins, D.
Jackson, B.A.
Jackson, Homer
Jackson, J.H.
Jackson, John B.
Jackson, L.H.
James, C.L.
Jameson, H.A.
Jamieson, John D.
Jamison, ?
Jarvis, John
Jeffries, H.R.
Jenkins, J.B.
Johnson, ?
Johnson, C.F.
Johnson, C.N.
Johnson, Chas. W.
Johnson, E.M
Johnson, J.E.
Johnson, Karl G.
Johnson, Milton
Johnson, R.A.
Johnson, R.E.
Johnson, Wm. L.
Johnston, Geo. W.
Johnston, W.S.
Jonarch Jr., Emil
Jones, C.C.
Jones, F.O.
Jones, Jas. M.

Jones, R.T.
Jordan, Roy
Kassel, Frank T.
Keith, G.
Keith, R.H.
Keller, ?
Keller, C.C.
Keller, Chas. E.
Kelley, D. Clarke
Kelley, E.P.
Kelley, J.J.A.
Kennedy, L.G.
Kensinger, J.L.
Kent, A.S.
Kepler Jr., David
Kepler, Jas. M.
Ketterman, R.C.
Kincaid, Robt. B.
Kline, E.B.
Kline, John
Knecht, Chas. A.
Knippenberg, J.P.
Krepps. W.B.
Krueger, A.W.
Kuchera, Wm. H.
Kurth, J.H.
Kussmann, H.J.
Kuy, F.S.
Kyle, J.H.
Laffler, Benj. E.
Laird, C.E.
Lakin, C.T.
Lamb, O.S.
Landrum, W.F.
Lange, L.S.
Langford, Chas. F.
Langley, Claude
Lashbrook, Chas. W.
Lasher, David

Latch, Harry
Latchem, C.G.
Lauterborn, Geo.
Layman, H.W.
Layton, W.J.
Ledbetter, Edw. J.
Leep, Thos. M.
Lefler, Lee E.
Lehman, Charley
Leitz, Wm.
Lernery, H.H.
Leslie, A.W.
Leslie, Vernon D.
Lessney, R.M.
Leverich, O.K.
Lewis, Jacob L.
Ligget, ?
Likes, G.C.
Lillich, Charles
Lillich, Harry
Lindhorst, O.F.
Lindsay, John A.
Link, G.R.
Little, C.B.
Lloyd, E.W.
Loebel, Richard
Loneland (Loveland?),
   D.E.
Long, Clude (Clyde)
Lord, John W.
Lorfing, Chas.
Lovelace, C.C.
Lovett, V.E.
Lowell, C.E.
Lowell, E.E.
Lumpkin, Joe
Luther, J.F.
Luther, Thos. L.
Lyle, Chas. E.

MacBride, H.W.
Major, Harold
Mailer, H.O.
Main, Lester G.
Mann, C.C.
Mapes, M.E.
Marley, P.
Marsh, Miles
Marshall, Warren
Martin, L.J.
Martin, W.A.
Martinson, C.A.
Mather, Geo.
Mathis, W.F.
Maule, R.P.
Mauls, F.E.
Maxwell, John A.
May, Ellis
May, W.C.
Maze, W.W.
McAndrew, J.L.
McArthur, C.R.
McBride, H.W.
McCallum, A.L.
McCallum, D.I.
McCallum, Homer D.
McCampbell, S.S.
McCarten, G.C.
McCarty, C. Wm.
McCarty, John C.
McCarty, Thos. W.
McCauley, J.E.
McCauley, Ralph R.
McCombs, Don C.
  Judge
McCras, H.Y.
McCready, C.E.
McCully, Chas.
McDonald, Jos. W.

McGann, Francis L.
McGin, J.L.
McGowan, Geo. F.
McKenzie, H.S.
McMurtrie, Kirk
  (McMurtire)
McNabb, A.F.
McNabb, L.B.
Mead, August H.
Mead, C.E.
Mendenhall, F.E.
Menturn, W.L.
Merry, W.Y.
Mertel, Fred H.
Meseraull, S.F.
Metz, E.R.
Meyer, Geo.
Michael, Chas. W.
Michel, Roy P.
Middleton, John W.
Milam, Glen E.
Milam, M.H.
Miler, Chas. C.
Miles, John S.
Miles, R.G.
Miller (Milier?), C.A.
Miller, B.F.
Miller, Chas. C.
Miller, E.P.
Miller, Frank W.
  (Millen)
Miller, G.H.
Miller, L.A.
Miller, Leon J.
Miller, R.E.
Miller, W.P.
Miller, William
Millis, E.R.
Minks, Jas. H.

Mitchell, M.D.
Mitchell, R.L.
Mitchell, W.W.
Modrell, Robt, C.
Moffett, O.D.
Moffett, W.E.
Moore, C.E.
Moore, Emmet B.
Moore, Ernest
Moore, J.V.
Moore, John A.
Moore, W.T.
Morris, G.F.
Morris, R.F.
Morris, R.O.
Morse, Wm. G.
Morton, A.J.
Moseley, Eugene
Moulton, Roy S.
Mueller, Robt. E.
Munsell, Alvin H.
Murphy, A.L.
Murray, John C.
Myers, Chas. C.
Nason, Frank C.
Nason, R.E.
Nave, C.L.
Neeley, Frank B.
Neely, John V.
Neil, W.J.
Nelson, A.L.
Nelson, C.F.
Nelson, Elmo J.
Nelson, W.H.
Neuelle, Floyd
Neugebauer, A.L.
Newitt, Fred D.
Newton, J.R.
Nicklin, J.E.

Nilson, C.R.
Norris, Al H.
North, S.L.
Northcutt, C.B.
Nugent, Michael
Numbers, A.R.
O'Hara, R.D.
Offutt, J.B.
Ogden, Thos. J.
Olson, D.H.
Onsen, M.C.
Overstreet, Harry L.
Owings, L.R.
Pains, S. Collins
Painton, R.T.
Palmer, Dudley R.
Palmer, Ray H.
Parker, E.R.
Parker, R.P.
Parrett, Lincoln
Parsons, L.J.
Patterson, W.H.
Paugh, I.F.
Paxton, R.A.
Payne, E.E.
Payne, Earl
Payton, J.E.
Pemberton, H.W.
Pendleton, F.N.
Pendleton, H.E.
Perkins, W.C.
Peterson, C.W.
Peterson, L.
Peterson, M.C.
Peterson, M.J.
Peterson, R.J.
Peterson, W.D.
Petzold, J.
Petzold, Walter

Phillips, R.E.
Phires, P.J.
Pinckney, A.W.
Pike, R.M.
Pipe, R.M.
Pitkin, Chas. W.
Pitts, C.A.
Plaskett, M.J.
Plumb, John H.
Pointer, Chas. E.
Port, Frank H.
Porter, Geo. H.
Porter, Lee, Jr.
Potter, Van S.
Powell, Otto
Powell, T.A.
Prather, L.C.
Price, A.D.
Price, E.D.
Price, Edwin H.
Price, Harry E.
Price, Jack
Prince, A.L.
Prosser, David H.
Pryor, J.A.
Puckett, M.T.
Purcell, W.E.
Purnell, W.J.
Purvis, R.A.
Quant, Chas. H.
Quick Jr., B.S.
Quinn, Wm. W.
Rankin, D.
Rankin, J.D. Kenneth
Ready, E.H
Reddell, Marion
Reddell, Roy A.
Redmond, Geo. J.
Reed, A.J.

Reed, O.B.
Reeder, J.I.
Reese, Geo. A.
Reeves, Jas.
Reichenecker, N.V.
Reitz, H.S.
Remaly, C.E.
Reppert, F.L.
Reynolds, A.L.
Reynolds, C.A.
Reynolds, G.Y.
Reynolds, Geo. S.
Rhoads, B.H.
Rhoads, C.P.
Rhodes, Dr. CR
Rhodes, Dusty
Rhodus, C.E.
Rhodus, W.R.
Richard, Fred V.
Richards, John
Richards, Wm. F.
Richey, C.E.
Richmind, T.V.
Rider, D.A.
Riley, E.E.
Riley, J.E.
Ring, Roy
Rives, Don
Robinson, David P.
Robinson, Ellis E.
Robinson, Roy I.
Rogers, Irving
Rogers, P.G.
Rogers, W.O.
Rohrbach, Wm.
Roney, Wm. J.
Roosa, Harris F.
Root, Archie W.
Root, Richard R.

Rose, R.W.
Roth, E.A.
Rowles, R.M.
Rugg, Hugh A.
Ryan, C.B.
Ryan, Dr. Ed. C.
Samins, S.J.
Sandstrom, C.M.
Sanford, Leroi
Sargent, Geo. W.
Sayers, M.
Schafer, R.R.
Schell, C.F.
Scherer, Geo. B.
Schill, Frank A.
Schlee, Willis
Schmidt, A.P.
Schmidt, Walter P.
Schneider, Ralph
Schuert, John
Schultz, H.B.
Schwarzhola, E.C.
Scott, W.H.
Scovill, F.L.
Seigmund, Roy E.
Self, W.H.
Sellers, Wm. A.
Semon, Fred A.
Seredge, (Sevedge?) J.O.
Serfor (?), G.L.
Seymour, J.E.
Seymour, J.U.
Shake, Edw. S.
Shares, J.T.
Sheets, Jas. P.
Sheppard, Lloyd E.
Sheriff, W.D.
Shipley, M.W.
Shoemaker, G.P.

Shrader, P.L.
Shrauger, Ira
Shreck, Edd. G.
Shryer, C.W.
Shueman, R.R.
Shuler, F.M.
Shupp, A.D.
Sillin, C.J.
Simmons, A.J.
Simmons, C.L.
Simmons, Wm.
Simons, A.H.
Simons, J.H.
Simons, V.A.
Small, E.D.
Smalley, Neil F.
Smith, A.P.
Smith, Albert J.
Smith, C.F.
Smith, C.J.
Smith, E.K.
Smith, G.A.
Smith, G.L.
Smith, H.L.
Smith, L.A.
Smith, L.D.
Smith, P.
Smith, Robt. V.
Smith, W.A.
Smith, W.W.
Smith, Wm. H.
Smyth, H.N.
Snodgrass, L.W.
Snyder, U.G.
Sofge, Fred
Soutto, G.T.
Soward, Olaf F.
Spake, Dr. B.A.
Spake, Edward

Sparks, C.F.
Sparks, Dr. J.W.
Sparks, Jos. L.
Sparks, Wm. O.
Spence, Wm. P.
Sprague, Leon C.
Spriesterbach, L.
Stahlman Jr., Geo.
Stalder, E.E.
Standerfer, H.
Standstrom, Gus A.
Staton, Edward
Staton, E.E.
Staton, Howard
Stegmaier, C.
Steinmetz, Chas.
Stevens, B.E.
Stevens, W.S.
Stewart, Chester B.
Stewart, Claude E.
Stewart, Jack,
Stillwell, E.Q.
Stockdale, Edw. E.
Stockdale, R.J.
Stone, Henry E.
Straight, H.M.
Stratton, E.L.
Stratton, E.N.
Strom, Robt. L.
Stuckey, A.T.
Stuckey, H.M.
Studebaker, M.C.
Studebaker, Ray
Suckys, S.
Sullivan, Harry L.
Summers, F.G.
Summers, R.A.
Swanson, John A.
Swartz, Harry M.

Swartzcope, F.W.
Talboth, I.J.
Taneyhill, Paul A.
Taneyhill, T.R.
Tanner, C.L.
Tanner, Chas. L.
Tanneyhill, CR
Tansey, Thos. G.
Tarry, Chas. E.
Tarry, L.W.
Tarry, Ray
Tatum, Geo. E.
Tauber, Bruno D.
Taylor, Frank A.
Taylor, Roy W.
Thomas, B.F.
Thomas, G.W.
Thomas, J. Earl
Thomas, R.G.
Thomas, R.L.
Thompson, Geo.
Thompson, H.L.
Thompson, Louis
Thompson, N.A.
Thompson, N.R.
Thorp, Harry B.
Thrutchley, B.H.
Tinklepaugh, H.O.
Townsend, Geo. F.
Trublood, Chas. S.
True, Floyd L.
Trueblood, W.E.
Truitt, Edw.
Turner, J.P.
Tuttle, V.M.
Tyrel, Cyrus
Underwood, H.W.
Underwood, V.
Van Fossen, C.W.

Van Fossen, F.E.
Vance, D.H.
Vetter, Geo. W.
Victor, Clarence
Vielhause, Theo.
Vullade, Geo.
Wacker, Geo. H.
Wade, John
Wador, John
Wagner, W.H.
Wait, J.L.
Wakefield, C.A.
Walker, Hy. J.
Walker, R.S.
Wallan, Russell
Walmer, H.
Walmer, Jas. E.
Walter, A.T.
Ward, C.W.
Ware, Earl B.
Warrell, P.A.
Washburn, K.W.
Washington, C.H.
Watkins, Lorenzo
Watson, A.B.
Watson, A.E.
Watson, J.W.
Watt, E.M.
Way, Carl
Way, Jas. H.
Weaver, I.I.
Webb, Thos. B.
Weber, Geo. E.
Weber, J.C.
Weber, John J.
Weber, W.F.
Weddle, F.E.
Weeks, R.B.
Weeks, Wm. M.

Weems, Levi M.
Welch, W.W.
Wells, C.E.
Wells, E.W.
Wells, O.M.
Wentling, Byron
Werner, Frank
Werner, John C.
West, G.C.
West, O.P.
Wheeler, Fred C.
Whisman, H.H.
Whitaker, Edwin C.
White, Carl T.
White, C.E.
White, Claude O.
White, E.L.
White, Fred (R. or B.)
Whitworth, R.E.
Wickliffe, L.A.
Wiggins, E.M.
Wiggins, Ralph
Wilber, Fulton
Wilds, E.E.
Wiles, Glenn
Wiles, J.F.
Wiles, W.G.
Wilkerson, Robt. J.
Wilkinson, J.W.
Williams, A.T.
Williams, Dallas L.
Williams, E.F.
Williams, Fred R.
Williams, Fred T.
Williams, Jas. H.
Williams, R.B.
Williams, W.H.
Williams, W.W.
Wilson, D.W.

Wilson, E.J.	Wolffing, R.H.	Wright, Clifford
Wilson, Edw. P.H.	Womack, I.E.	Wright, Geo. T.
Wilson, Elmer W.	Wood, S.A.	Wright, L.E.
Wilson, R.A.	Wood, Wm. L.	Wright, Walter
Wilson, R.J.	Woodruff, D.K.	Wyant, Deane J.
Wilt, Jack	Woodrull (Woodruff?),	Wydick, Rufus S.
Wilts, L.G.	I.L.	Yarton, John F.
Winchell, J.E.	Woods, A.O.	Yoakum, W.A.
Winchell, L.A.	Woods, J.H.	Young, F.H.
Wingate, J.C.	Woods, John L.	Young, John
Wingate, W.N.	Woods, William "Bill"	Zahn, Fred
Winter, Alvin A.	Woodward, H.G.	Zeller, John L.
Wohlford, J.W., Jr.	Woolsey, A.F.	Zimmerman, H.E.
Wolfe, Wm. D.	Wright, W.J., Jr.	Zimmerman, I.R.

KLAN OCCUPATIONAL STATUS COMPARISON

An occupational status comparison of Klan and non-Klan workers draws a sharp distinction between the two classes of Kansas City citizens. Occupational status is the esteem society and the U.S. Census Bureau assign to different jobs.

4.4 percent (N=39) of the Klansmen were employed in high, nonmanual status, white-collar occupations such as attorney, clergyman and physician. Only 1.7 percent of Kansas City's male workforce enjoyed high, nonmanual status.

24.1 percent (N=216) of the Klansmen were middle, nonmanual status workers. This class included small-business owners, managers and public officials, among others. 5.5 percent of the non-Klan workers appeared in middle, nonmanual occupations.

26.9 percent (N=240) of Kansas City Klansmen worked in low, nonmanual status occupations. This category comprised clerks, public servants and salesmen. 14.8 percent of the general workforce was classified as low, nonmanual.

19.3 percent (N=173) of the Kluxers were skilled, blue-collar craftsmen such as railroad engineers, carpenters and machinists. 17.6 percent of Kansas City's non-Klan workers were also skilled workers.

19 percent (N=169) were apprentices or semiskilled workers. These Klansmen worked as switchman, brakemen and meter readers, among other occupations. 23.2 percent of the city's other workers toiled at this level.

3.2 percent (N=29) of Kansas City Klansmen were unskilled laborers. This number contrasts starkly with the 24.5 percent of the total male population who appeared in the same category. Additionally, 3.1 percent (N=28) of the Klansmen were either retired or unemployed.

The most common Klan occupations, as represented by the "average" Klansman introduced earlier, were small-business owner, clerk and railroad engineer; that is, middle, nonmanual, low, nonmanual or skilled work occupied most Klansmen. Among the occupations the Klan did not attract were banker, industrialist and fundamentalist Christian preacher.

The middle-class character of Klan members noted by contemporary reporters becomes even more evident when the high, middle and low nonmanual white-collar workers and the skilled, blue-collar craftsmen are combined. This number, 668, or 74.7 percent, is Wyandotte Klan No. 5's "middle-class quotient." The middle-class quotient of the entire working male population of Kansas City in 1920 was 39.6 percent. The middle-class quotient of those ineligible for Klan membership—Catholics, Jews, non-whites and the foreign born—was 19.4 percent. Native-born white males were closest but trailed the Klansmen at 49.3 percent.

The Kansas City Klan members' middle-class quotient remains high when compared to Klan members across the county despite differences of geography and economy. The middle-class quotient of Aurora, Illinois, for example, was 79 percent; Denver, Colorado, 70 percent; and Richmond, Indiana, 75 percent. Across the nation, otherwise normal middle-class Americans responded to the Klan's message of white, native-born Protestant revival.

Occupational Status

HIGH NONMANUAL (N=39)

Architect	1	Editor	1
Attorney	5	Judge	1
Chemist	1	Optometrist	1
City officials	1	Superintendent	1
Clergyman	6	Teacher	1
Dentist	8	Veterinarian	1

MIDDLE NONMANUAL (N=216)

Businessmen

Automobile dealer	1		Welding	1
Automobile repair	1		Draftsman	3
Automobile supply	2		Embalmer	1
Baker	2		Farmer	2
Barber	8			
Baseball Management	1		*Inspectors*	
Bicycle dealer	1		Animal	11
Candy store	1		Engineer	1
Cleaner	1		Oil	1
Coal dealer	4		Unspecified	4
Creamery	3			
Diner	3		*Managers*	
Druggist	13		Assistant	4
Dry goods	3		Business	7
Electric	1		Cemetery	1
Equipment	1		Department	5
Furniture	3		General foreman	1
Garage	5		Railroad	1
Grocer	24		Sales	49
Mortician	1			
Nursery	1		*Public Officials*	
Painter	1		Asst. co. attorney	1
Photography	1		Asst. supt. B.O.E.	1
Plumber	5		Chief clerk	1
Printer	1		City abstractor	1
Real Estate	4		County assessor	1
Roofing	1		County clerk	1
Salvage	1		County coroner	1
Serum	2		Marshal	1
Shoe repair	1		Sheriff	1
Shoe store	4			
Tinner	1			
Tobacco	1			
Transfer	3			
Typesetting	2			
Unspecified	15			
Warehouse	1			

LOW NONMANUAL (N=240)

Agent	5	Security officer	1
Bookkeeper	16	Sheepbuyer	1
Clerk	81	Soda jerk	1
Collector	7	Student	3
Dispatcher	1	Telegraph operator	1
Floorman	1	Timekeeper	4
Foreman	36	Yardmaster	4
Mailman	3	Weighmaster	1
Spectacular	1		
Teller	1		

Public Servant

Fire captain	2	
Police captain	1	
Dep. co. clerk	2	
Dep. marshal	1	
Detective	2	
Junior clerk	1	

SKILLED (N=173)

Baker	3
Boilermaker	5
Bricklayer	1
Butcher	8
Cable splicer	1
Carpenter	27
Car repair	1

Salesman

Advertising	2	Electrician	14
Automobiles	5	Engineer (RR)	33
Bakery	4	Fireman (RR)	15
Battery	1	Fitter	2
Cream	2	Harnessmaker	1
Electric	3	Hostler	1
Film	1	Jeweler	1
Grocery	1	Lineman	2
Insurance	8	Machinist	23
Investments	1	Mechanic	10
Meat	5	Painter	3
Mill	1	Planer	1
Oil	1	Plasterer	5
Real Estate	2	Plumber	3
Shoes	2	Printer	3
Tires	1	Roofer	1
Traveling	4	Shoe repair	3
Unspecified	19	Sign painter	1
		Tinner	3
		Toolmaker	1
		Welder	1

SEMI-SKILLED (N=169)

Apprentice	1	Millhand	1
Barber	5	Motorman	1
Bellhop	1	Oiler	1
Boxmaker	11	Operative	1
Brakeman	16	Operator	3
Brander	1	Parts chaser	2
Caller	1	Pilot (RR)	1
Chauffeur	12	Policeman	7
Fire dept. chauf.	1	Repairman	1
Police dept. chauf.	4	Stiller	1
Conductor	13	Switchman	16
Cook	2	Trimmer	2
"Employee"	53	Under Sheriff	1
Fireman	6	Waiter	1
Fireman (private)	1	Watchman	6
Gateman	1		
Hostler helper	1	UNSKILLED (N=29)	
Marker	1	Laborer	29
Machinist helper	1		
Meter reader	2	UNKNOWN OR RETIRED (N=28)	
			28

NOTES

Introduction

1. Suits, *Hugo Black of Alabama*, 411; Chalmers, *Hooded Americanism*, 26–27, 31; Hamby, *Man of the People*, 114; Gordon, *Second Coming of the KKK*, 130–31; Lay, *Invisible Empire in the West*, 8; Rives, "Tom Baird," 144; Chalmers, 286–87; Charles McBrayer, interview with author, 1992; Rives, "Klan on the Kaw," 29.
2. Chalmers, *Hooded Americanism*, 8, 18–20, 26, 28–29, 31; Charles McBrayer, interview with author, 1993; Rives, "Klan on the Kaw."
3. Harcourt, *Ku Klux Kulture*, 2, 108, 110, 144–45; *Ligonier (PA) Echo*, June 15, 1927.
4. Harcourt, *Ku Klux Kulture*, 28–29.
5. Ibid., 26.
6. Ibid., 30; Simmons, "How I Put Over the Klan," 32.
7. Chalmers, *Hooded Americanism*, 31–32.
8. Ibid., 104.
9. Ibid., 33.
10. Ibid.; Duffus, "Salesmen of Hate"; Shepherd, "Ku Klux Koin"; Chalmers, *Hooded Americanism*, 38.
11. Kansas, State v. Knights of the Ku Klux Klan, *Plaintiff's Abstract of the Record*: 41; 139–40; Chalmers, *Hooded Americanism*, 34.
12. *Plaintiff's Abstract, passim*.

NOTES TO PAGES 27–38

Chapter 1

13. Higham, *Strangers in the Land*, 159; Goldberg, *Discontented America*, 140–42, 159–60.
14. Larry Hancks, ed., "A History of Kansas City, Kansas, Municipal Government" (unpublished manuscript, Wyandotte County Historical Museum, Bonner Springs, Kansas), 3–5.
15. Ibid.
16. Ibid.
17. Fink, *Workingmen's Democracy*, 113; Carman, *Foreign Language Units of Kansas*, 526, 531, 894; Manzo, "Sequent Occupance in Kansas City, Kansas," 23–24.
18. *Kansas City (KS) Kansan*, March 6, 1927.
19. Fink, *Workingmen's Democracy*, 122–24.
20. *American Eagle*, February 16, 1894.
21. Hancks, "History of Kansas City, Kansas," 11–12; Landis, *Kansas City's Mayors*, 37–39.
22. Hancks, "History of Kansas City, Kansas," 13–14; Landis, *Kansas City's Mayors*, 88; Katie Cowick, *Story of Kansas City*, 17.
23. *Kansan,* June 18, 1922.
24. Ibid.
25. Ibid.
26. Ibid., January 25, 1921; June 18, August 14, 27, December 31, 1922.
27. Rives, "Klan on the Kaw," 6.
28. Ibid.
29. Ibid.
30. Ibid., 7.
31. Ibid.
32. Ibid.
33. Ibid., 8.
34. Ibid.
35. Ibid.

Chapter 2

36. Ibid.
37. Ibid.
38. *Kansan,* July 24, 1921.

39. Rives, "Klan on the Kaw," 9.

40. Ibid.

41. *Kansan*, April 24, 1922; Rives, "Klan on the Kaw," 9.

42. Ibid.

43. Ibid., 9–10.

44. Ibid. 10

45. Ibid.

46. Ibid.

47. Ibid.

48. Ibid.

49. Ibid.

50. Ibid.

51. Ibid., 11.

52. Ibid.

53. *Plaintiffs Abstract*, 50–51, 101.

54. Rives, "Klan on the Kaw," 11; *Manning (SC) Times*, April 12, 1922; *Delphos (KS) Republican*, May 15, 1924.

55. Rives, "Klan on the Kaw," 11; Evans, "Klan's Fight for Americanism," 56.

56. Rives, "Klan on the Kaw," 11.

57. Ibid., 11–12.

58. Ibid.

59. Ibid.

60. Ibid.

61. Ibid.

62. Ibid., 12–13.

63. Ibid., 13.

64. Ibid.

65. Ibid.

66. Ibid.

67. *Kansan*, May 8, 1922; Rives, "Klan on the Kaw," 13.

68. *Catholic Register*, May 11, 1922.

69. Rives, "Klan on the Kaw," 13–14.

70. Ibid., 14.

71. Ibid.

72. *Catholic Register*, May 11, 1922.

73. Ibid., July 1927; *Kansan*, January 3, 1924.

74. Rives, "Klan on the Kaw," 14–15.

75. Ibid., 15.

76. Ibid.

77. *Kansas City (KS) Weekly Press*, November 3, 1922.

78. Rives, "Klan on the Kaw," 15.

79. Ibid.

80. Ibid., 16.

81. *Joplin (MO) Globe*, April 3, 1923; Rives, "Klan on the Kaw," 16.

82. Ibid.

83. Ibid.

84. Ibid.

Chapter 3

85. Ibid., 17.

86. Ibid.

87. Ibid.

88. Ibid., 18; *Kansan*, November 14, 1923.

89. Rives, "Klan on the Kaw," 18.

90. *Catholic Register*, November 9, 1922; Rives, "Klan on the Kaw," 18.

91. Rives, "Klan on the Kaw," 18–19.

92. Ibid., 19; *Plaintiff's Abstract*, 45, 50.

93. Rives, "Klan on the Kaw," 19; *Kansan*, March 28, April 7, 1923.

94. *Springfield (MO) Leader and Press*, February 23, 1923.

95. *Kansas City (KS) Globe*, January 20, 1915; June 14, 1916; *Kansas City (KS) Press*, June 29, 1923; April 25, 1924.

96. Rives, "Klan on the Kaw," 19.

97. *Kansan*, June 13, 1922.

98. Ibid., July 28–29, 1926.

99. Ibid., October, 22, 1916; September 18, February, 22, 1924; October 20, 1925.

100. Rives, "Klan on the Kaw," 19.

101. *Kansan*, October 16, 1925. Summers lived at 646 Troup and 549 Greeley in a short period of time. Both were located in white neighborhoods.

102. Rives, "Klan on the Kaw," 19–20.

103. "Ku Klux Klan of Wyandotte Co. Klan" to Jonathan M. Davis, September 30, 1923, Governors Papers, Kansas Historical Society.

104. John L. Zeller, Wyandotte Klan No. 5, to Jonathan M. Davis, July 18, 1923, Governors Papers, Kansas Historical Society.

105. Rives, "Klan on the Kaw," 20.

106. Ibid., 20–21.
107. Ibid., 21.
108. Ibid.
109. Ibid.
110. State of Kansas, *Report of Cases* VXL, 182–87.
111. *Kansan*, March 14–15, 1927.
112. Rives, "Klan on the Kaw," 22.
113. Ibid.
114. Ibid.
115. Sloan, "Kansas Battles the Invisible Empire."
116. Rives, "Klan on the Kaw," 22.
117. *Kansan*, August 14, 1922.
118. Rives, "Klan on the Kaw," 23.
119. Ibid.
120. Ibid., 23–24.
121. *Kansan*, May 1, 1922.

Chapter 4

122. Rives, "Klan on the Kaw," 24.
123. Ibid.
124. Ibid.; Knights of the Ku Klux Klan (Kansas), "Application for Charter," May 3, 1923, Records of the Office of the Secretary of State, Kansas Historical Society.
125. Rives, "Klan on the Kaw," 24.
126. Knights of the Ku Klux Klan (Kansas), "Constitution and By-Laws of the Knights of the Ku Klux Klan," May 1, 1293, Records of the Office of the Secretary of State, Kansas Historical Society.
127. Rives, "Klan on the Kaw," 25.
128. Minute Men of America, "Application for Charter," (1925), Records of the Office of the Secretary of State, Kansas Historical Society; Lay, 60–61.
129. Chalmers, *Hooded Americanism*, 261.
130. Knights of the Ku Klux Klux Klan (Kansas), "Charter," "Application for Charter," August 4, 1924, Records of the Office of the Secretary of State, Kansas Historical Society.
131. *Topeka (KS) Daily Capital*, October 31, 1922.

132. Bishop Augustus J. Schwertner, Diocese of Wichita, to John Malone, state deputy Knights of Columbus, May 9, 1923, James Malone Papers, Kansas Historical Society.

133. Rives, "Klan on the Kaw," 26.

134. Ibid.

135. Gertrude A. Sawtelle to Jonathan M. Davis, August 20, 1924, Governors Papers, Kansas Historical Society.

136. Monk and Reed, *Veil of Fear*.

137. *Kansas City (KS) Gazette*, May 26, 1896; *Kansas City (KS) Catholic*, August 9, 1894.

138. *Gazette*, August 11, 1894.

139. *Lucas (KS) Independent*, September 22, 1926.

140. *Gazette*, April 24, 1896; *Kansas City Catholic*, June 14, 1894.

141. *Anti-Catholic Crusader*, March 1914.

142. Nordstrom, *Danger of the Doorstep*, 46–47.

143. Rives, "Klan on the Kaw," 27.

144. Evans, "Ku Klux Klan's Fight," 34, 38, 52, 54; Charles McBrayer, interview with author, August 1993.

145. Ibid., 9.

146. Grant, *Passing of the Great Race*, 39–41.

147. *Klankraft in Kansas*, n. l., September 1927. Kansas Historical Society.

148. C.P. Rhoads to Ben S. Paulen, January 30, 1925, Governors Papers, Kansas Historical Society.

149. Arkansas City, Kansas, Ku Klux Klan to C.E. St. John, September 8, 1922, Kansas Historical Society.

150. Rives, "Klan on the Kaw," 28.

151. *Garnett (KS) Republican-Plaindealer*, September 4, 1923.

152. Ibid.; *Fort Scott (KS) Tribune and Monitor*, September 13, 1923.

153. James Malone to Bishop John Ward, Archdiocese of Kansas City, Kansas, May 5, 1923, James Malone Papers, Kansas Historical Society.

Chapter 5

154. Rives, "Tom Baird," 144.

155. Ibid., 145.

156. Ibid.

157. Ibid.

158. Ibid., 146–47.

159. Ibid., 148, 153.
160. "Ku Klux Klan List," Henry J. Allen Papers, Library of Congress.
161. Rives, "Klan on the Kaw," 32.
162. Ibid.
163. Ibid., 33.
164. Ibid.
165. Ibid.
166. Ibid.; *Kansan*, May 4, 1925; January 30, 1927; August 20, 1922.
167. Rives, "Klan on the Kaw," 33.
168. Ibid., 34.
169. Ibid.
170. *Kansan*, May 21, 1921; April 16, 1922; Rives, "Klan on the Kaw," 34.
171. Ibid.
172. Ibid.
173. *Kansan*, September 19, 1924; *Bonner Springs (KS) Chieftain*, September 18, 1924.
174. Rives, "Klan on the Kaw," 34.
175. Ibid., 35.
176. Ibid.
177. Ibid.
178. Ibid., 29.
179. Ibid., 30.
180. Ibid.
181. Ibid.
182. Ibid.
183. Ibid.
184. Ibid.
185. Ibid.
186. Ibid., 31.
187. Ibid.
188. Ibid.; *Kansan*, October 30, 1922.
189. Rives, "Klan on the Kaw," 31.
190. Chalmers, *Hooded Americanism*, 105.
191. *Fredonia (KS) Daily Citizen*, March 24, 1923.
192. Rives, "Klan on the Kaw," 31.
193. Ibid.
194. Ibid.

Chapter 6

195. Ibid., 37.
196. *Weekly Press*, December 14, 1894.
197. Rives, "Klan on the Kaw," 36.
198. Ibid., 36–37.
199. *Kansan*, clipping, 1925.
200. See Appendix A.
201. Rives, "Klan on the Kaw," 37.
202. Ibid., 37–38.
203. Ibid., 38.
204. Ibid.
205. Ibid.; Delgadillo, *Crusader for Democracy*, 169–70; 175.
206. Rives, "Klan on the Kaw," 37.
207. Ibid., 38.
208. Ibid.
209. *Southwest News*, March 12, 1925.
210. Rives, "Klan on the Kaw," 38.
211. Ibid., 40.
212. Ibid.
213. Ibid.
214. Ibid.
215. Ibid.
216. Ibid.; *Kansan*, 12, 15, 1926.
217. Ibid.
218. Rives, "Klan on the Kaw," 40.
219. Ibid., 8.
220. Ibid., 41.
221. *Kansan*, September 14, 1926.
222. Rives, "Klan on the Kaw," 40.
223. Ibid.
224. Ibid.
225. Ibid., 41.
226. Ibid.
227. Ibid.

Chapter 7

228. *Kansas City (MO) Times*, December 7, 1951.

229. Ibid., Rives, "Klan on the Kaw," 41.

230. Ibid.

231. Ibid., 42.

232. Chalmers, *Hooded Americanism*, 171–72.

233. Rives, "Klan on the Kaw," 42; *Kansan*, January 1, 1928. *Crusaders* was alternately spelled *Krusaders*.

234. Chalmers, *Hooded Americanism*, 283; Delgadillo, *Crusader for Democracy*, 175.

235. *Kansan*, September, 16, November 16, 1927.

236. *News-Review*, July 30, 1928.

237. *Chillicothe Constitution-Tribune*, December 17, 1928.

238. Rives, "Klan on the Kaw," 44.

239. Bill Greggs, treasurer, Wyandotte County Historical Society, to Tim Rives, September, 18, 2013.

240. Rives, "Klan on the Kaw," 44.

241. *Weekly Press*, December 14, 1894; *Gazette*, April 24, 1896.

242. Rives, "Klan on the Kaw," 44; Hamby, *Man of the People*, 114; Suits, *Hugo Black of Alabama*, 411.

243. Rives, "Klan on the Kaw," 44-45.

244. Ibid.; Harry obituary, January 13, 1969, clipping, North Platte, Nebraska, Public Library; Robin Garlett, St. Patrick's Church, North Platte, Nebraska, to Tim Rives, June 19, 1923.

245. Rives, "Klan on the Kaw," 45.

246. Ibid.

247. Ibid.; *Kansan*, October 16, 1925.

248. Rives, "Klan on the Kaw," 38, 45; Civic League of Kansas City to Charles B. Griffith, December 7, 1923, Governors Papers, Kansas Historical Society.

249. Rives, "Klan on the Kaw," 42.

250. *Times*, December 7, 1951.

251. Rives, "Klan on the Kaw," 42-43.

252. Ibid.

253. Ibid.

254. *Times*, January 3, 1952; Rives, "Klan on the Kaw," 43.

255. Ibid.

BIBLIOGRAPHY

Primary

Ben S. Paulen Papers, Kansas Historical Society.
Henry J. Allen Papers, Library of Congress.
James Malone Papers, Kansas Historical Society.
Jonathan M. Davis Papers, Kansas Historical Society.
Kansas, State v. Knights of the Ku Klux Klan. *Plaintiff's Abstract of the Record*. Topeka, KS: n.d.
Kansas, *Report of Cases Argued and Determined in the Supreme Court of Kansas*. Topeka, KS: State Printing Plant, 1924.
Records of the Office of the Secretary of State, Kansas Historical Society.
Supreme Court of Kansas Records.

Newspapers

American Eagle (Kansas City, KS)
Bonner Springs (KS) Chieftain
Catholic Register (Kansas City, MO)
Chillicothe (MO) Constitution-Tribune
Delphos (KS) Republican
Fort Scott (KS) Tribune and Monitor
Fredonia (KS) Daily Citizen

Garnett (KS) Republican-Plaindealer
Iola (KS) Anti-Catholic Register
Joplin (MO) Globe
Kansas City (KS) Advocate
Kansas City (KS) Catholic
Kansas City (KS) Kansan
Kansas City (MO) Star
Kansas City (KS) Sun
Kansas City (MO) Times
Kansas City (KS) Weekly Press
Klankraft in Kansas
Ligonier (PA) Echo
Lucas (KS) Independent
Manning (SC) Times
News-Review (Roseburg, OR)
Southwest News (Lakin, KS)
Springfield (MO) Leader and Press
Topeka (KS) Daily Capital
Topeka (KS) State Journal

Articles

Duffus, Robert L. "Salesman of Hate: The Ku Klux Klan." *World's Work* 46 (May 1923).

Evans, Hiram W. "The Ku Klux Klan's Fight for Americanism." *North American Review* 223 (May 1926).

Shepherd, William G. "Ku Klux Koin." *Colliers* (July 21, 1928).

Simmons, William J. "How I Put Over the Klan." *Colliers* (July 14, 1928).

Secondary Sources

Carman, J. Neale. *Foreign Language Units Kansas: Historic Atlas and Statistics*. 2 vols. Lawrence: University of Kansas Press, 1962.

Chalmers, David M. *Hooded Americanism: The History of the Ku Klux Klan*. Durham, NC: Duke University Press, 1994.

Cowick, Katie. *The Story of Kansas City*. Kansas City, KS: Central High School Press, 1924.

Delgadillo, Charles. *Crusader for Democracy: The Political Life of William Allen White*. Lawrence: University Press of Kansas, 2018.

Fink, Leon. *Workingmen's Democracy: The Knights of Labor and American Politics*. Urbana: University of Illinois Press, 1983.

Frost, Stanley. *The Challenge of the Klan*. Indianapolis, IN: Bobbs-Merrill, 1924.

Goldberg, David J. *Discontented America: The United States in the 1920s*. Baltimore, MD: Johns Hopkins University Press, 1999.

Gordon, Linda. *The Second Coming of the KKK: The Ku Klux Klan of the 1920s and the American Political Tradition*. New York: Liveright Publishing Corporation, 2017.

Grant, Madison. *The Passing of the Great Race*. New York: Charles Scribner's Sons, 1916.

Hamby, Alonzo L. *Man of the People: A Life of Harry S. Truman*. New York: Oxford University Press, 1995.

Hancks, Larry, ed. *A History of Kansas City, Kansas, Municipal History*. Bonner Springs, KS: Wyandotte County Historical Museum, n.d.

Harcourt, Felix. *Ku Klux Kulture: America and the Klan in the 1920s*. Chicago: University of Chicago Press, 2017.

Higham, John. *Strangers in the Land: Patterns of American Nativism*. New Brunswick, NJ: Rutgers University Press, 1988.

Landis, Margaret. *Kansas City's Mayors: A Look Back*. Kansas City: n.p., n.d.

Lay, Shawn, ed. *The Invisible Empire in the West: Toward a New Historical Appraisal of the Ku Klux Klan in the 1920s*. Urbana: University of Illinois Press, 1992.

Manzo, Joseph. "Sequent Occupance in Kansas City, Kan.—A Historical Geography of Strawberry Hill." *Kansas History* 4 (Spring 1981).

Monk, Maria, and Rebecca Reed. *Veil of Fear: Nineteenth-Century Convent Tales*. West Lafayette, IN: NotaBell Books, 1999.

Moore, Leonard J. *Citizen Klansmen: The Ku Klux Klan in Indiana, 1921–1928*. Chapel Hill: University of North Carolina Press, 1991.

Nordstrom, Justin. *Danger on the Doorstep: Anti-Catholicism in the Progressive Era*. Notre Dame, IN: University of Notre Dame Press, 2006.

Rives, Tim. "Klan on the Kaw: The Ku Klux Klan in Wyandotte County, Kansas." *Historical Journal of Wyandotte County* 3, no. 14 (Winter 2015–16).

———. "The Ku Klux Klan in Kansas City, Kansas, 1921–1930." Master's thesis. Emporia State University, Emporia, Kansas, 1995.

———. "The Second Ku Klux Klan: Rise and Fall of a White Nationalist Movement." https://pendergastkc.org/article/second-ku-klux-klan-kansas-city-rise-and-fall-white-nationalist-movement.

———. "Tom Baird: A Challenge to the Modern Memory of the Kansas City, Monarchs." In *Satchel Paige and Company: Essays on the Kansas City Monarchs, Their Greatest Star and the Negro Leagues*. Edited by Leslie A. Heaphy. Jefferson, NC: McFarland & Company, 2007.

Sloan, Charles W., Jr. "Kansas Battles the Invisible Empire: The Legal Ouster of the KKK from Kansas, 1922–1927." *Kansas Historical Quarterly* 4 (Autumn 1974).

Suits, Steve. *Hugo Black of Alabama: How His Roots and Early Career Shaped the Great Champion of the Constitution*. Montgomery, AL: NewSouth Books, 2005.

INDEX

ABOUT THE AUTHOR

Tim Rives is the deputy director and supervisory archivist of the Eisenhower Presidential Library, an army veteran and a Kansan. He is a graduate of Wichita State University and Emporia State University. His articles have appeared in *The Journal of Military History*, the *Baseball Research Journal* and *Prologue*, among others. His work has been translated into Turkish.

Visit us at
www.historypress.com